I0005210

——YOUR——
Privacy &
Security

John Minges

Copyright 2014, John Minges.

All rights reserved. No parts of this book may be reproduced or transmitted in any form or by any means without the expressed written permission of the author. Requests for permission should be addressed to john@minges.com.

Your Privacy and Security
ISBN: 978-0-9905990-0-5

This book is for information purposes only and not intended to take the place of legal or professional advice. The author, as well as the publisher, assumes no liability or responsibility for the use or misuse of the information contained herein. Due to the wide variety of individual circumstances, neither the author nor publisher warrants or guarantees that the information provided is applicable or advisable for any situation.

Cover and interior design by Stephanie Whitlock Dicken.

All rights reserved worldwide.

～

*I would like to thank my wife, soulmate
and best friend, Sarah, for her time
in reading, editing and encouraging me
to write a little more. I love you!*

～

～

I would like to recognize and thank those who helped me in my journey writing this book. Without your time and collective effort reading and re-reading various draft copies, while giving me critical feedback, I would not have been able to move forward. Thank you to everyone: Donna Ashley, Ricky Ellis, Jeffrey Feinman, Kip Gaskins, Virginia Hardy, and Phil Howard. I would also like to thank those who worked hard in the edit and design process for this book. Thank you to Bethany Bradsher, Stephanie Dicken and Carla Nielsen. I could not have done this without you all!

～

Table of Contents

PREFACE   13

INTRODUCTION   17

CHAPTER 1
Personal Protective Measures   23
Reality • Crime Prevention • Paying Attention • Simple
Action Steps • Offering Solutions • The New World:
What Has Changed? • So, What is Real and What is
Just Imagined?

CHAPTER 2
The Beginning   37
It Starts at Birth – DNA Sample • Our Patterns & Choices •
Accepting Truth • Privacy, What Privacy? • Peek-A-Boo –
I Can Find You!

CHAPTER 3
Technology   43
Hacking Globally • Fusion Centers • "Pre-Crime"
Surveillance Cameras • Aerial Surveillance • Micro Air
Vehicles • Eye Scan Biometrics • Your Fingerprints •
Molecular Scanners • RFID – Radio-Frequency
Identification • Electronic Thievery • All Individual
Financial Data Records • Currency Tracking •
Airport Tracking

CHAPTER 4

Glimpse Into The Future   59

Smart Television • The Smart Grid • Solar Flares or EMP • Cyber Attack Threat • Money Talks – The Secret! • Currency Transaction Report • Suspicious Activity Reporting Requirements • Safety Deposit Bank Boxes • Personal Identifiers • Facial Recognition • Automated License Plate Readers • The Black Box • No Need To Say Hello! • Become AWARE! • Say Cheese! • Special Delivery • Tracking People, Pets or Vehicles • Making a Simple Photocopy

CHAPTER 5

Your Life   81

Can You Opt Out? • What You CAN and SHOULD Do! Telephone Risks • National Do Not Call Registry – Telemarketing Calls • Opting Out – Prescreened Offers of Credit and Insurance • Junk Mail – DMA Opt Outs • Financial Institution Privacy Statements • Credit Freeze • Data Broker Opt Outs • FERPA – Family Educational Rights and Privacy Act - Opt Out

CHAPTER 6

Online Security   93

WE Do It To Ourselves! • Surfing Privacy Online • Keeping Secret Passwords Secret • Online Shopping • Warranty/Registration Cards • Removing Your Online Footprint • Cookies – Not The Kind You Eat • Spam – Spoof – Phishing • Additional Online Protection • Wireless Encryption • Computer and Cell Phone Disposal • Peek-A-Boo – I See You! • Computer Theft

CHAPTER 7

A Blanket of Security   105

Shopping Tips • Store Loyalty Cards – Carrot or Stick? • Your Wallet • Cash And Carry • ATM/Debit Card Security • The Boogie Man • Our Sixth Sense or Gut Feelings • Curious George • Trash or Treasure • Shred Fest • Stop Check and Document Fraud

CHAPTER 8

Identity Theft   119

The Unthinkable Happens • Review Your Credit Card
Statement • Protecting Your Wealth – Investments •
Social Security • Paper or Plastic – Cash or Credit • Lost
Money • Escheat and Unclaimed Property • Pensions •
Tax Refunds • Mortgages • Savings Bonds

CHAPTER 9

Home Security   131

Found Your Dream Home? • Next Steps • Natural Hazards •
Environmental Hazards • Insurance • Have a CLUE What
You Are Getting Into! • Ignorance is Bliss • Action Steps •
A Hidden Advantage • A Safe Room • Anti-Climb Paint •
Operation Identification – Proactive Deterrent • Happy
and Sad Occasions • Answering Machine Safety • Mailbox
Safety • Let There Be Light • Fencing • Driveway Safety •
Garage Security • Open Sesame • Basement Doors And
Windows • Crawl Space Doors • Fireplace Ash Doors •
Storage Sheds

CHAPTER 10

Safety Around the House   163

Outdoor Grilling • Pool Safety and Security • Home
Sweet Home • The Big Picture • Locks • Hiding Keys •
Look First Beware of Scams • Common Ruses • The
Invited Stranger • Keeping You Secure • Where Did I Put
My Keys? • Windows and Glass • The Weakest Link

CHAPTER 11

When You Were Away   181

Who Is Mr. Burglar? • Hidden In Plain Sight • Safes:
Real or Imagined Protection? • How Important Are The
Valuables You Want To Protect? • Fire Protection or
Burglary • Security Safes • Beware of Dog!

CHAPTER 12
Security Systems - The Electronic Watchman   193
Questions to Ask • Types of Systems • False Alarm •
Cameras and DVR • Additional Camera and DVR
Questions to Consider • The Life-Saving Moment •
Questions to Ponder • Keep Bedside

CHAPTER 13
Fire Safety and Protection   207
Kitchen Fires • Have a Fire Plan • Home Fire Prevention
Tips • Fireplaces and Wood Stoves • Clothes Dryer Fires •
Become as Lint Free as Possible • The Smell of Danger –
Smoke Detection • Fire Extinguishers

CHAPTER 14
Other Ways to Ensure Home Safety   217
Home Inventory • Storage Unit Security • Protecting Your
Home From Flooding • The Cut-Off Quiz • Call Before
You Dig! • Apartment or Condo Living • Elevator Safety

CHAPTER 15
Automobile Safety   225
What Should You Carry? • Driver's License and
Registration Privacy • Are You Being Followed? •
Carjacking • Combat Parking • Car Security Devices •
Valet Parking and Car Washes • Unattended Trailer or Boat

CHAPTER 16
Travel Safety   233
Travel Pride • Traveling Overseas • Preparing to Leave •
Luggage •Travel Insurance • Rental Car Security and
Insurance • Your Money or Your Life! • Pick Pocketing •
Looking Good

CHAPTER 17
Hotel Safety   249
Choosing Your Room • Hotel Fire • Hotel Room Doors
and Locks • Bed Bugs • In-Room Safes – Are They Really
Safe? • Hotel Trash Can • Hot Tub and Pool Dangers

CHAPTER 18
Preparedness – What Does This Mean to You? 259
The Basics • Early Warning System • Basic Survival •
Breathe Deep • Water – Take Immediate Action • Food •
Waste Not, Want Not • Shelter • Sanitation •
Medical Needs • Evacuation Plan • Closing Comments

Preface

For a long time I have had a voice deep within me, a voice that has prodded my soul to finally share my thoughts, personal experiences and the vast amount of research I have collected over the years concerning personal privacy and home security.

Beyond this book, I know that I have several other books waiting to be written. Yet, like a lot of folks I've made many excuses, procrastinated and ignored these feelings for a long time. Turning fifty has made me realize even more than before that time is important. For those that say fifty is middle aged, I can't help but wonder how many one-hundred-year-old friends they actually have? So, the time to act is now!

Since early childhood, I have recognized two passions that continue to recur throughout my life. The first is a deep caring concern I've always had for strangers and for those in need. The help I give is not out of pity or guilt, but from an overarching sense of obligation I have always felt towards my fellow man. Unfortunately, I believe that many people are so busy worrying about taking care of themselves and their families that they ignore everything else around them. I don't fault anyone for this, yet I have come to realize that my life is much more enjoyable if I focus on others rather than myself.

I have indeed been blessed in so many ways – beyond having financial means. I have visited many wonderful places around the world and experienced more than most dream about in their lifetime. This has allowed me to have an incredibly fulfilling life, for which I am thankful. This also has allowed me to see the world in a different light.

Another important part of my life has to do with my faith in God. While I'm not an outwardly religious person, I know firsthand God's strength and power. He has sustained and strengthened me in the difficult times of my life. I also know that regardless of what I do here on earth – no matter how "good" I might try to be – I cannot "earn my way" to heaven. Thankfully, it has already been provided to me through my faith in Him. What a gift!

The second passion I've had for as long as I can remember is an interest in all things related to law enforcement. I've had the pleasure of serving on various state boards and commissions, volunteering for local nonprofits and even serving as an elected county official. I also have had the privilege of meeting many people who are experts in their respective fields – local and statewide law enforcement, fire rescue personnel, private investigators and many more. This book will attempt to incorporate their collective knowledge with my experiences and present all this to you in a usable form.

Taking the time and energy to write and publish this book has not been easy, and it has been a struggle at times to get the words on paper. But I am reminded that all this is not by accident but by design, so without any further ado I would like to introduce to you my first book: *Your Privacy and Security*.

Introduction

I'm sure that every generation thinks that the world in which they live is fraught with more danger than the generation before. By far one of the biggest threats we face today is that of normalcy bias and choosing to live a life of apathetic existence versus engaging in life's challenges with interest.

Normalcy bias is a psychological state of mind whereby people who are facing possible disaster tend to discount or ignore the probability of its occurrence or the outcome such a disaster may bring.

It appears that many people have made a conscious choice to live their lives in a narcissistic manner. Their focus is what they can get from life versus what they can contribute. In addition some people believe in making others, specifically the government, into the responsible party to take care of ALL their needs rather than having any sense of obligation to help themselves. This can be an extremely dangerous situation that has the potential to turn a seemingly civil society into a chaotic mess, especially when a crisis occurs. How quickly do you think our society would unravel if no one took responsibility to help those in need? What happens when people become hungry?

The truth is that in society today most people strive to take the path of least resistance and have become lazy and indifferent to the world around them. Sadly, a large majority has come to believe the lie that has been perpetuated many times over – that most things are beyond our control, which is not true. When a person chooses to sit back and do nothing, that in and of itself is a choice, but we ignore our apathy and keep telling ourselves we can't do anything about it.

While we may not be in total control of every aspect of our lives, this does not mean we have abdicated our responsibilities as individuals to others for them to dictate not only our present circumstances, but our future as well. Far from it!

Instead, our lack of control in some areas should make us more diligent in our efforts to maintain as much independence as possible, so that we can direct any outcome toward our favor or, at the very least, have a say in what we think is right and just. It appears today that the vast majority of Americans cheerfully accept the back-seat approach to life. People are totally content to watch things happen rather than make them happen.

Another tragic mistake that is corroding the fabric of our lives occurs daily, as people accept an attitude that portrays them as a victim of life. When a negative circumstance occurs, you will likely find someone happy to take up the banner proclaiming that what happened was unjust. Individuals willingly point to every negative aspect of their life as "proof positive" that they are forever wronged. Sadly, in many cases there appears to be a complete failure on the part of individuals to take responsibility for their own lives. It becomes easier to default to the notion of proclaiming what has been "done to them" versus what "they are doing to themselves" when obstacles arise. When others try to point out the duty of personal responsibility, they are met with harsh criticism and claims of being biased or unconcerned for the less fortunate.

The assumption by many – that all outcomes are predetermined – is a complete falsehood! It's time for everyone to take responsibility for their own lives, to stop complaining about what they feel is injustice and concentrate on seeking the equal justice that is afforded to all. The idiom is true: you have to "take the bull by the horns" and deal with what you face head on if you expect it to change! Change doesn't happen on its own; you have to make it happen.

Playing the role of victim in life serves no purpose, other than giving you an excuse to wallow in self-pity. While your life might not be easy, and circumstances are sometimes very difficult, no one promised that everything would be easy, so get over it. Life is not always fair! Yet, how you choose to view life is and forever will be in your control. Making the best of all situations never hurt anyone.

No matter where you are, there is opportunity around you, but you must be willing to search it out and strive to achieve your best. Life is made up of ALL experiences, not just the good ones, and what occurs each moment is a learning opportunity.

In writing this book, I realize that everyone's thoughts and concerns about privacy and security are different. We each have a different perspective and come with different experiences. Regardless of these differences, nothing prevents you from quickly and accurately assessing your own situation and thinking more critically about where you live and your overall surroundings. Your actions or inactions have consequences.

In order to get the most out of this book, you will need to set some time aside not only for reading, but also for putting what you have learned into practice. By doing so, you will be able to diminish the opportunity for the criminal element to be successful in attempting a home invasion, loss of personal property or threat of bodily harm.

This book is meant to be an eye-opening window to the reality of the world around you. What you learn will likely surprise some and shock others. This book is also meant to be a "practical guide" to help the average person be proactive rather than only reactive when it comes to your privacy and security.

I hope that as the reader you will be driven by factual information instead of acting out of fear. Taking responsibility for your own safety and security is not just a right but a privilege. This book can be, for you, the first of many steps in a lifelong journey toward attaining personal safety.

CHAPTER ONE
Personal Protective Measures

We don't live in a lawless land, and the vast majority of people we come in contact with each day are law-abiding citizens. But what should you do if you find yourself in a situation where your life is in danger? For most people, the two automatic reactions are either fight or flight. Both of these reactions are valid, and only you can determine what is right for each situation. However, note that there is nothing wrong with doing everything possible to remove yourself from a dangerous situation! It is the prudent and wise thing to do.

It is important that you are aware of your surroundings at all times, no matter where you are or what time of day or night it might be, no matter how many times you go to the same grocery store or travel to the same gas station. Remember, every moment in time is different and circumstances can change instantly.

Most of us have enough awareness of our surroundings to sense that certain situations might be dangerous, and it is obviously in your best interest to avoid these situations. However, it is a fact of life that there are occasions when danger finds us. What happens if you have to use force? Do you use lethal force or less than lethal force? The answer to this question is really a simple one: Do you feel your life is being threatened?

No matter your position on gun control or how uncomfortable it might be for you and your loved ones to talk about the use of force, this is a conversation you must have.

It is my strong belief that everyone needs to have some form of personal protection and know how to use it. For some this involves the use of a firearm, while for others this may mean a different approach.

Fortunately, for most of us in America, we do not live in an environment where we feel our lives are threatened on a daily basis. Living in such an environment would not be much of an existence. Yet I think it would be a fair assessment to say that many people now feel that we live in a time with more threats to our personal safety than ever before.

It is still legal in America for you to own a firearm. It is unclear if this will remain a right in the future. Laws vary greatly from state to state, so before you make your choice of what you are comfortable carrying – be it a firearm or other protection device like pepper spray – you need to check with your local law enforcement to make sure it is legal.

For whatever reason, people ignore the fact that laws governing firearms only apply to the law-abiding citizens willing to adhere to them. Of course, the criminal element among us could care less about the law. You will never be able to stop the criminal element from possessing or using firearms to commit violent acts, no matter what laws are passed, and to think differently is extremely foolhardy.

If you are in the camp that wants to make an argument that guns kill people, then you need to use the same logic in talking about all motor vehicles.

The reality is that the drunk driver, through his or her individual choices and actions, is what kills a victim, not specifically the vehicle itself. The person who pulls the trigger is responsible for his action and the tool he uses could be a gun or a baseball bat. Yet I don't hear of anyone wanting to ban all baseball bats.

Individuals are responsible, not the methods they choose, period!

A law-abiding citizen who obtains a permit that subjects them to a background check to purchase and/ or legally carry a firearm is not a threat to anyone except the criminal seeking to do them harm. These citizens are much like those who have taken a driver's test to drive a car.

Beyond the typical handgun or shotgun, a wide range of personal protection devices is available to help law-abiding citizens protect themselves. Probably one of the most common and widely accepted personal protection devices is pepper spray. This nonlethal method can, *in some cases*, deter a would-be attacker and give the victim enough time to run and escape to safety. One brand you might want to consider is made by Kimber®, a company that offers a product called PepperBlasterII.[1]

Another product that has greater stopping power than pepper spray is a Taser®[2]. This has been typically utilized by law enforcement, but a consumer version is now available to individuals for purchase. A background check is required before you are given a code to activate the device. Instead of arming themselves directly, some people choose dogs as a means of protection. Regardless of the method you choose to protect yourself this must be accompanied with a fervent mindset that takes your own personal safety seriously.

It would be nice to think that we live in a bubble and that only good things happen. I also realize that it is stressful to ask someone to constantly stay aware of your surroundings. Unfortunately, the vast majority of people will probably never carry a personal protection device, but those that do have adjusted their thinking and made a determination that they are better protected with carrying something than without it. However, don't be fooled into thinking that just because you have pepper spray buried in your purse or behind a pile of papers in your glove box that this is adequate protection. If you think this, then you are sadly mistaken! Also, don't think that you can count on the pistol you purchased and loaded ten years ago and placed in the drawer of your bedside table. If you have never fired it, how do you know if it works, or whether you could hit anything with it if it did?

Personal protection is more than just owning a piece of equipment. There are plenty of treadmills sitting idle, but those who never step on them don't wonder at the end of the day why they are not in shape or not losing weight. So stop fooling yourself, if you are, and take on the responsibility to set up time to train and learn how to use what you have to protect yourself.

Reality

If you ever hear a news report that a deadly shootout took place between the police and a perpetrator, you will likely hear the reporter comment about how many rounds were fired, and people will quickly comment on how this is excessive.

First, it is easy to be critical if you have never shot a gun. Be thankful if you have never been in a situation where you felt your life was in danger.

Second, if your life is threatened your body acts naturally and you experience a massive adrenaline dump. If you were protecting yourself with a firearm, would it matter to you the number of rounds you had to fire? Would you want more or less? Remember it is only a matter of seconds in which you have to react. Even if you have trained and shot firearms on a regular basis, being in a situation where you feel your life is in danger changes everything!

Crime Prevention

Law enforcement responds to crime and does its best to create an atmosphere to discourage incidents from happening in the area. However, neither law enforcement nor we ourselves have the capability of actually "preventing crime" from occurring. What we can and should do is actively seek to deter it from happening. This process needs to be ongoing and not just a one-time effort.

Typically there are three elements present for crime to occur. First there is the offender who has a specific desire to act, next there is an identified target that is available and, lastly, there is the opportunity for the crime to occur.

As you continue to read, think about these three aspects that take place and the steps you can take to prevent yourself or your property from being identified as a target. Are there things you can do to lessen the opportunity?

By far one of the biggest obstacles to safety today is complacency or security apathy by individuals. You need to understand that true safety and security is a lifestyle choice, not a one-time punch list.

Paying Attention

It would be nice to offer a few trite words of encouragement with a comment like, "You just need to be alert," or "aware," as an attempt make you feel better. Yet this honestly would be a disservice to you, the reader. Just saying these words and not providing information of why this is important does nothing to convey the full intent of the message. Let me explain.

Recently, while sitting in the airport waiting for my flight, I was struck by the fact that in general it appeared that everyone around me had become part of a nation of "zombies." It was like each person had become their own little space ship with their shields up and heads buried into their "smart phone" that was making them deaf, dumb and blind!

People walked around inside a dark airport with sunglasses on and ear buds in total oblivion to the life that surrounded them as they passed by. I'm convinced more than ever that we have become a nation of attention deficit hyperactivity disorder (ADHD) junkies!

Because of this phenomenon, it is important to be aware of your surroundings. A real key to personal security is exercising your brain power versus associating personal security primarily with physical strength. *I want to challenge you to train your brain to pay attention to life around you versus ignoring it!*

Simple Action Steps

When you get in your car you should fasten your seat belt immediately; knowing this is one activity you can do to help prevent injury in case of an accident. Most of us grew up being told at some point the need for, and benefit from, using a seat belt, and we accept this, either ignoring the warning or heeding the advice. Yet, there is an important distinction I'd like you to recognize. As most of us buckle up, we don't fear being in an accident or getting a traffic citation for not doing so. We just know in our gut that this is the right thing to do. This feeling inside is exactly the attitude I hope you will carry deep within you as you continue exploring this book.

As you begin thinking about putting into practice the recommendations outlined, I hope you start to feel empowered. Try to let your actions flow freely and become second nature, versus overthinking everything and getting too wrapped up in the "what if" scenarios.

I remember being told a long time ago that constantly thinking about any one subject can drive a person crazy, no matter how positive that subject. Recognize this, and if you start to feel overwhelmed slow down and take a break. Nothing is requiring you to hurry up and finish the next sentence, because I can assure you this was not written in one day. Remember the old saying that slow and steady wins the race!

Offering Solutions

Searching for the information you need and being aware of your surroundings should not instill one ounce of fear into your life. The opposite should be true!

You need to know that there are practical solutions to most of the problems you face. Your search for the truth ultimately should give you a real confidence and peace of mind, knowing that you are in fact outwardly doing what is necessary to discourage others from thinking that you are an easy target.

Realize, however, that as you actively go about seeking to find the right answers for your situation you will unfortunately encounter many companies advertising security products and services based totally on promoting fear. I contend that everyone needs honest information so they can trust in their abilities to think, act and prepare themselves for whatever circumstances that may occur. They don't need someone trying to sell them something.

As you read this book, you will be able to easily and quickly put into action the suggestions provided to improve your life and better protect not only yourself, but your loved ones as well. This should be a breath of fresh air for you to enjoy, not something to dread!

This book is not about buying something to make you feel or be safe as much as it is about YOU becoming more aware of what it means to be safe. Obviously everyone's situation is different; therefore, it will be up to you to determine how much of this information you can use and feel comfortable putting into practice.

A word of caution: In reading any book that goes into the specific details, it is easy to look at all the suggestions and quickly get overwhelmed with a long "to do" list, only to come back a week or month later and find nothing has been done. Please don't fall in this trap. I suggest you start slow and read each topic as if it were a stand-alone document.

Try to put into place something you have learned first before reading the next section. I realize, for some, this might seem like a painstakingly slow process, but I'd rather you implement one or more of the suggestions to help improve your personal safety and security than none at all. I strongly suggest you read, and then re-read this book. Feel free to literally get a pen to highlight points you want to come back to revisit. Realize that in order to be successful this must be YOUR plan of action, not someone else's.

I think it is important to state emphatically that there will be certain recommendations for specific products and/or services; however, no product, service or website I mention has in any way contacted me in advance or asked me to promote their product or service.

My recommendations are my own and come from my experiences of either personally purchasing and/or using the products or services mentioned or by doing a great deal of research and consulting with the experts to find the best available solution for the specific problem at hand.

Unfortunately, I cannot guarantee that you will be fully satisfied if you choose to purchase any product or service mentioned herein, because I simply can't be aware of every situation that might exist. However, the goal of this book is to simply try to convey and disseminate as much information as possible so you can determine the appropriate action to take to help make you and your family more secure.

The New World – What Has Changed?

The last time I checked, most people in the United States live in a home, not a bunker. Society as a whole has not broken down, and we are not currently seeing mass riots or civil unrest, yet!

If you look hard, however, you will find gated communities in a few larger cities. These are typically pockets of very wealthy individuals with large and luxurious homes. The neighborhood is exclusive, and many times it is surrounded by a fence or brick wall. Yet in most cases the additional security typically offered is only superficial at best. You might see an unarmed security guard stationed at an entrance casually monitoring the access of who enters the neighborhood. Sometimes visitors and delivery vehicles are asked to check in and sometimes not. During the day and night a private security force might be patrolling the area.

Obviously, the general public cannot afford to pay for a private security force and expect local law enforcement to handle all the duties of keeping the public safe. Also, people want to "feel safe" without being bothered or having to do anything extra. Some people have actually been known to call and complain if they see a police car in their neighborhood. People wonder if anything is wrong, versus being glad to see a law enforcement presence.

Every day we are confronted with new potential threats, both big and small. As you continue to read this book we will outline many of the threats you face and give you practical advice on how to protect yourself.

So, What is Real and What is Just Imagined?

I think it is important at the start to say what this book is NOT about! I do not personally believe that the world as we know it will for whatever reason come to an abrupt end, with a total societal collapse that spirals us into a state of anarchy.

Regardless of what happens, people adapt and I don't see everyone giving up their day job to go "bug out" to some remote destination to live the remainder of their lives off the land and become quasi-Amish. If you happen to be Amish please don't take offense, but note that the rest of the world isn't likely to adapt to your simple way of life.

I do, however, strongly believe that the future generations of Americans will be forced to live an entirely different way of life. In short, the future has been mortgaged, with no clear ability to pay back what is owed. At some point a total reset will have to occur and everyone will endure hardship. When this will happen is anyone's guess. Many people claiming to know the answer are either guessing, lying, trying to scare you or worse, trying to sell you something!

The main focus of this book will be about living today in the present, rather than focusing on what might come in the future. Focusing on your present situation does not mean, however, you get a pass to ignore the future, but it will definitely give you more time to prepare for it.

It will be up to you to pay close attention to what is happening in the world around you. To do this you need to read daily from various sources you trust to understand what is occurring around the world. Every source is slanted toward a specific bias, so take what you read and measure that with your own judgment of the truth and act accordingly.

You probably will quickly find that real truth typically comes in small doses and the rest is just meaningless chatter. Don't expect to be spoon fed, because finding out what is happening beneath the surface is not easy. All this is important because you will need to be able to quickly learn to adapt to the new reality in the event any significant change occurs, versus being stuck in your same routine wondering what happened.

The word picture comes to mind of a "deer in the headlights." If you have witnessed this, the deer appears to be frozen in time from fear of the unknown and the fear of the brightness of the light. Your job is not to remain frozen, but to know when to move and further realize that the brightness of the light can be your friend if you understand the source. Again, knowing what to do and when to do it is paramount to your survival; the time to learn is not in the midst of the crisis but NOW!

In many ways we have become totally numb and we fail to see things as they actually are, but continue to view the world as it once was. Accepting the reality of the present situation will be a difficult process. It will require you to change some of your lifelong habits and, quite frankly, your thoughts about life, which without question will be an extreme challenge for most people.

Some parts of this book will be driven by personal opinion; however, these opinions are based on facts derived from research. I am not just pulling something out of total thin air and asking the reader to believe it as truth. In many cases you will see a notation with a source has been stated for the material given. These sources are stated for a reason. I not only want, but expect, the reader to do their own research and come up with their own conclusions. Make sure any suggestion given is right for your situation. Trust but verify.

Recognize that when you read a book of this nature it is normal to experience a sensory overload from all the information that is contained herein. I totally understand that neither you nor I can prepare for everything bad that might happen in our lives. I also know that we simply must do our best and try not to worry about the rest, but let's face it, we all do. This is all part of what I think it means to be human.

We are all limited in the amount of time and personal resources we have to focus on any project. In dealing with privacy and security we all will automatically default back to ranking, in order of importance, the threats we openly acknowledge. However, there will be additional concerns we will likely discover in this process. The next step will be to develop a plan, at least in our mind, of how we will deal with each specific threat. Getting from the thoughts in our mind to actual action is another step that takes discipline.

The single greatest gift you can give yourself at this point is to remain open to change as you continue to read. I want this to be a gut check for you. Some of this information will likely resonate, while other bits and pieces may not, and that is OK. Regardless, take what you can use and create an action plan to implement the steps needed and keep reading. In the end I think you will be glad you did, and you will truly be satisfied in all that you have accomplished.

CHAPTER TWO
The Beginning

What makes you, you? When you were born you were given a name. This was the start of identifying who you are as a person, with likely the first official paperwork generated being your birth certificate. The proud parent or grandparent who posted your picture online for the world to see inadvertently started your online profile before you were even a year old! But what really makes someone unique is much more than a piece of paper, an online photo or even our habits, likes and dislikes. What makes us unique is our DNA.

It Starts At Birth – DNA Sample

Recently a US Supreme Court ruling allowed law enforcement to collect DNA samples from people arrested, but not yet convicted of serious crimes. Rest assured that this sample will likely be stored in the FBI's Combined DNA Index System (CODIS) database, which is the largest DNA database in the world and, as of 2011, held nine million records.

However, what most people are totally unaware of is that a law was passed in 2008 making DNA screening for newborns mandatory! The following information comes from an article about the program on www.aclu.org[3]:

> "The DNA of virtually every newborn in the United States is collected and tested soon after birth. There are some good reasons for this testing, but it also raises serious privacy concerns that parents should know about.
>
> States require hospitals to screen newborns for certain genetic and other disorders. Many states view the testing as so important that they do not require medical personnel to get parents' expressed permission before carrying it out. To collect the DNA sample, medical personnel prick the newborn's heel and place a few drops of blood on a card. There is one question that new parents rarely ask: What happens to the blood spots after the testing is done? This is where newborn screening becomes problematic.
>
> It used to be that after the screening was completed the blood spots were destroyed. Not anymore. Today it is increasingly common for states to hold onto these samples for years, even permanently. Some states also use the samples for unrelated purposes, such as in scientific research, and give access to the samples to others."

So think about this for a moment. From the time you are born a DNA sample is going to be taken, without any parental consent needed, and it will likely be stored indefinitely in a government database.

Our Patterns & Choices

We define ourselves by our actions, and others define us by our reputation and the people with whom we associate. In any case, our life is made up of a combination of these factors and is influenced by the personal decisions we make on a daily basis.

Somehow we have convinced ourselves that life just happens to us! Unfortunately, we have come to believe in total randomness versus stopping to observe how much of a role we play in what actually occurs. If anything, this should make you stop and think for just a moment. Look at the beauty of nature, including the plants and insects around you; do you think this is really just all random, or is it possible there is a defined order to what you see?

As humans, we are no doubt much different than all the other creatures on earth in that we can direct our steps and have many choices. What if you made the choice to take a different path? To stop just letting things happen to you, but make them happen? Life would be totally different, don't you think?

The basis of this book is to provide you with facts. These facts will be presented in a way that hopefully will tell a story. However, this story is one of truth over fiction. It is important that you as the reader recognize that all this is not just personal opinions or preferences, but factual truths that have been discovered by doing lots of research and talking to experts. Layers upon layers of information have been carefully sifted and condensed into what is contained here.

Accepting Truth

Learning the truth should NOT make you feel uncomfortable. If it does then you need to question why. What about the truth concerns you? There are lots of different choices we make in our life that determine our destiny. Each day stands alone, and it is up to us to make sure we are making the best of that day. The truth can hurt, but its power does not have to forever remain hurtful. The more we know, both positive and negative, the better informed we can become to make the decisions we need to make to live our lives to the fullest.

Privacy, What Privacy?

It would be nice to think that we live in an age that respects our rights and privacy. America is a wonderful and special country to live in. In many cases we have been brainwashed to believe that all the other countries in the world want to be like us, whatever "like us" means in our own mind. Likewise, our view of individual privacy is inexplicably tied to what we know as personal freedom. Average Americans may or may not have a passion for freedom or understand its cost, but nonetheless they will eventually become very vocal if they think "their rights" are being trampled on.

Peek-A-Boo – I Can Find You!

If you live in the United States you may or may not know that your home has likely been photographed on more than one occasion and you can access this information to see a street view and even a satellite view.

This picture shows in great detail how your home looks as well as what is located in your backyard. It may show your car parked in your driveway, or it could even disclose your license number. What you may not know is that Google™ recently agreed to pay a $7 million settlement that covered thirty-eight states including the District of Columbia after admitting that it had intercepted e-mails, passwords and other information over unprotected wireless access while snapping pictures of your home street view. Oops!

CHAPTER THREE
Technology

As technology advances it opens new and exciting doors, allowing us to achieve greater things. But it also opens the door for more abuses, delving more deeply into our personal lives.

Many people are ignorant and some choose not to believe that the United States government can and is actively being intrusive into our personal lives, in effect knowing every detail. Why would it matter, you might wonder, and why would they care? The lines between fact and fiction seem to be blurred. Any mention of Big Brother and his all-knowing and seeing eyes quickly puts you into the category of being one of the tin-foil-hat, conspiracy-theorist nut jobs.

But if you are interested in facts versus fiction then you need to know the truth. The question is, however, are you willing to accept the truth?

Every keystroke can be and is recorded; every e-mail and Internet search can be traced to the original source computer. A National Security Administration computer program called XKeyscore accomplishes this with great ease and efficiency.

Conversations, including those on either hardwired or wireless phones, can be heard and recorded. We are indeed living in a unique and interesting time. We can choose to fear the unknown or embrace it and adapt to it. Now more than ever we need to not only understand the truth but also to stop pretending that it does not exist.

To back this statement up one only has to look and read a 2012 article by James Bamford on www.wired. com.[4] This article gives specific details of a massive complex near the small town of Bluffdale, Utah, built for the National Security Administration and known simply as the Utah Data Center. The total size of this $2 billion complex of buildings is an amazing one million square feet of space. However, even more amazing is what takes place inside.

The article states the following: "Flowing through its servers and routers and stored in near-bottomless data-bases will be all forms of communication, including the complete contents of private e-mails, cell phone calls, and Google searches, as well as all sorts of personal data trails – parking receipts, travel itineraries, book-store purchases, and other digital 'pocket litter.' But 'this is more than just a data center,' says one senior intelligence official who until recently was involved with the program. The mammoth Bluffdale Center will have another important and far more secret role that until now has gone unrevealed. It is also critical, he says, for breaking codes. And code-breaking is crucial, because much of the data that the center will handle – financial information, stock transactions, business deals, foreign military and diplomatic secrets, legal documents, confidential personal communications – will be heavily encrypted. According to another top official also involved with the program, the NSA made an enormous breakthrough several years ago in its ability to crypt analyze, or break, unfathomably complex encryption systems employed by not only governments around the world but also many average computer users in the U.S. The upshot, according to this official: 'Everybody's a target; everybody with communication is a target.'"

While the acronym NSA officially stands for National Security Administration, others in the field use this acronym to remind themselves to "Never Say Anything." This information in and of itself should be amazing, especially when you really stop to think how significantly this could impact your life. While there is nothing practical you can do about this intrusion into your personal privacy, it is always better to be well informed than blissfully ignorant to the facts of life. Your life and everything you do is "pocket litter" to the government.

I have two simple questions I would like to pose to the reader at this point. What determination is used to identify the enemy? At what point do YOU become the enemy?

Hacking Globally

The daily use of computers for communication, coupled with wireless technology, has enabled the increasingly popular surveillance technique of hacking. Instead of trying to intercept a call via wiretapping, the surveillance organization, be it governmental or independent, would surreptitiously load a software program on the target's source computer or other wireless device and monitor all video, audio and any other electronic data that is received or transmitted. A researcher by the name of Bill Marczak, who works with a company called Citizen Lab that "focuses on advanced research and development at the intersection of digital media, global security, and human rights," estimated that the selling of this type of software is now a $5 billion business![5]

There are many countries around the world that don't have the capability to develop their own in-house sophisticated software that can go undetected. So they go out and search the marketplace for an off-the-shelf solution, and they are not disappointed. One such vendor is a U.K. based company called Gamma Group that has developed a suite of products called FinSpy. Another company based out of Milano, Italy, is aptly called Hacking Team. Surprisingly, this company has opened an office in the United States and is marketing directly to law enforcement agencies.

It is no surprise that governments globally are continuing to ramp up their spying efforts. A group called the Electronic Frontiers Foundation used the Freedom of Information Act to obtain redacted records from the FBI concerning their surveillance programs and stumbled upon the term "remote operations unit" printed on a document. Upon further investigation, via looking at resumes on LinkedIn™, subcontractors were identified as having worked in dedicated units in the

United States government and verified that these units do have the capability to remotely hack into computers and monitor information without being detected.[6]

Fusion Centers

I realize as you continue to read you might find yourself becoming skeptical. I think it is common to want to believe that all the technology out there will be used ONLY to catch the bad guys, and that all of this really has nothing to do with you. Why would anyone care about what you are doing or what your political or religious beliefs might be anyway?

Well, we have all heard that information is power and we also know that, when unchecked, absolute power has a tendency to become corrupt. Even with the use of technology there still has to be a means whereby information can be gathered locally, as well as at the state level, and finally disseminated to the federal government. One such method is through something called a fusion center. According to Wikipedia, the free encyclopedia: "A fusion center is an information sharing center, many of which were jointly created between 2003 and 2007 under the U.S. Department of Homeland Security and the Office of Justice Programs in the U.S. Department of Justice.

They are designed to promote information sharing at the federal level between agencies, such as the Central Intelligence Agency (CIA), Federal Bureau of Investigation (FBI), U.S. Department of Justice, U.S. military, and state and local level government. As of

July 2009, the U.S. Department of Homeland Security recognized at least 72 fusion centers. Fusion centers may also be affiliated with an Emergency Operations Center that responds in the event of a disaster.

The fusion process is an overarching method of managing the flow of information and intelligence across levels and sectors of government to integrate information for analysis. *That is, the process relies on the active involvement of state, local, tribal, and federal law enforcement agencies – and sometimes on non-law enforcement agencies (e.g., private sector) – to provide the input of raw information for intelligence analysis. As the array of diverse information sources increases, there will be more accurate and robust analysis that can be disseminated as intelligence (emphasis mine).*

A two-year senate investigation found that "the fusion centers often produced irrelevant, useless or inappropriate intelligence reporting to DHS, and many produced no intelligence reporting whatsoever." The report also said that in some cases the fusion centers "violated civil liberties or privacy."[7]

Regardless of the above facts, 72 fusion centers are part of a bigger overall blueprint known as the National Criminal Intelligence Sharing Plan (NCISP). This organization was formed in 2002 as part of the Global Intelligence Working Group (GIWG), which serves as the group that coordinates information for both law enforcement and justice organizations. Supposedly the overarching goal of these centers is the actual gathering and analysis of intelligence as a tool to investigate and hopefully prevent and/or deter possible criminal activity.

"Pre-Crime" Surveillance Cameras

The United States-based BRS Labs, which stands for Behavior Recognition Software, is just one company that is taking video surveillance to a completely new level with their proprietary program they call AISight®. This software program is unique in that it empowers a camera to not only monitor an area, but to distinguish between normal activity and suspicious behavior that deviates from the imputed norms. Furthermore, this surveillance capability can actively monitor the movement of up to one hundred individuals at any given time. What is even more impressive is its ability to build a literal historical "memory" of behaviors for the area monitored.[8]

At this point I can't help but think of the phrase that states a person is innocent until proven guilty. However, the future might define innocence in a completely different way than we define it today. With this technology you may be "guilty" based solely on the perceived intent of your actions.

Aerial Surveillance

An Ohio-based company called Persistent Surveillance Systems developed a product in 2008 that can be placed on the outside of an airplane that flies at ten thousand feet for hours on end. The information gathered by the device, which is called Hawkeye, gives law enforcement the capability of viewing the entire goings-on of any city at a glance, both in real time and replayed on demand by transmitting the images to a ground-based surveillance command center. This technology has been deployed for use in cities like Philadelphia, Baltimore and Compton, California, as well as for events such as NAS-CAR. It is said that this system cannot read license plates or see faces, but it can and does track movements with ease.[9]

Micro Air Vehicles (MAVs)

Surveillance technology of today seems to only be limited by our ability to dream. Builders are making smaller and lighter bug like surveillance drones that can blend into everyday surroundings. This is all part of The United States Air Force Office for Science Research, which serves as the exclusive research arm for the United States Air Force. Their role focuses on being on the cutting edge of technology to make the Air Force of the future look nothing like it does today! The Assistant Secretary of Defense for Research and Engineering focuses on six areas of science carrying out this mission that include: Metamaterials and Plasmonics, Quantum Information Sciences, Cognitive Neurosciences, Synthetic Biology and Computational Modeling of Human and Social Behavior. The development and use of micro air vehicles is literally just the beginning of what is to come.

Eye Scan Biometrics

An old English proverb states, "The eyes are the windows to the soul," and while this may be true, the future could see the use of our eyes as a password to everyday living.

Starting in 2007, the West Virginia University Center for Identification Technology Research (CITeR), in conjunction with the FBI's biometric facility, began working on technology to capture the image of a person's iris at distances of fifteen feet to as far as two hundred yards! This is obviously a great covert tool to use, but let's switch gears for a moment so that I can ask you a question. Have you been to the eye doctor lately? If you have, then you likely have submitted to have your eyes tested for glaucoma, which by all means is a good thing. However, in doing so, a picture was taken of your eyes, which was likely stored and submitted to the IRIS™ (Intelligent Research in Sight) Registry. "The IRIS Registry is the nation's first electronic health records-based comprehensive eye disease clinical registry, which enables ophthalmologists to monitor and improve patient care, while also generating data to compare the efficacy of treatments and comply with government reporting requirements."[10]

So, is this really to be used for your good, or could this possibility be yet another intrusion to your personal privacy? You can decide. Lastly, just so you can understand one possible use of this current technology, one can look at the United Arab Emirates, which has, as an option, the use of an "iris passport" for traveler identification.[11]

Your Fingerprints

Long gone are the days of the typical police ink blotter rolling your fingerprint on a card to enter the data into the FBI database. Today fingerprint technology, like all other technologies, has advanced greatly. One company on the forefront is the Huntsville, Alabama-based company IDair. This company, which was founded in January 2011 by Advanced Optical Systems, Inc. (AOS), has created an impressive technology called AIRprint™, which is a rapid, long-range fingerprinting device that can actually read your fingerprint from a distance of twenty feet away!

Molecular Scanners

You might have noticed that airport security seems to be in a constant state of change when it comes to scanning the passenger. We have gone from walking through a metal detector and receiving a pat down to a full X-ray body scanner. However, a radical change is on the way, due in part to a company called In-Q-Tel which works with the Central Intelligence Agency and others to provide the latest technology. In-Q-Tel has introduced a device called a molecular scanner which, according to the company, can be activated from 164 feet away from the individual in question and tell the operator basically everything they might want to know about the individual's body, clothes or luggage.[12] This device will identify traces of drugs or gunpowder on your clothes, measure adrenaline body levels and supposedly be able to tell you what the person had for breakfast – all without laying one finger on the person. Amazing!

RFID - Radio-Frequency Identification

You need to realize that RFID microchips, with

their mini antenna, can and likely will be embedded in *everything* in the not-too-distant future! If it moves, you will be able to track it and link it to the person holding it.

If you stop and think for a moment about the possibilities, it can be staggering. The future will see a refrigerator that tracks and monitors what you eat and maybe generates a shopping list for you. You will pop your microchipped dinner in the microwave oven and it will automatically warm the meal to the correct temperature.

What you wear, what you read, and where you go all can be tracked and stored. This information could be sold to companies who then will try to influence your buying patterns. RFID devices will make your home "smarter" by integrating the technology allowing devices to "talk to one another." You might think this is far-fetched, but think again.

The future is already here for many applications. Think about the "SpeedPass" device you have on your car for the toll booth. If you have gone to the library recently, did the book have to be deactivated before you could check it out? Did you wave your credit card like a magic wand over the card reader to pay for your purchases at your local fast food restaurant? Corporations will likely tell you not to worry, because RFID tags are only used to monitor inventory and prevent theft. However, the truth paints a different picture.

If you go online to a company called RetailNext (www.retailnext.net) and search a few of the pages on their website, you will read the following:

"RetailNext takes advantage of all potential sources of data to give you a full picture of the factors that can lead to success and improvement in your retail locations. Now you can combine the available intelligence from almost limitless data sources including:

- Video feeds
- POS systems
- WiFi
- RFID tags
- Kiosks
- Digital signage
- Time-and-attendance systems
- Task management
- Staffing schedules
- Third party traffic counting systems
- External sources such as promotional calendars or weather reports.

These factors together give you the most complete picture of how many people enter your stores, where they go, what they look at, and how it all connects to their actual buying behavior. And our open, flexible system lets you add new data sources as they become available."[13]

Hopefully you noted from the above list the mention of WiFi. This is a little reminder that your smart phone does a lot more "talking" on its own than you might think by transmitting data about you without you even being aware of it!

By now you should not be surprised, but hopefully you are beginning to be aware of just a few of the realities happening in the world around you.

Electronic Thievery

Today most credit and debit cards have been embedded with Radio-Frequency Identification Chips (RFID) or Near Field Communication (NFC) chips. Unfortunately, having these devices in your cards can pose a security risk. The process is known as skimming, or electronic pickpocketing, and it involves using an RFID transponder to electronically swipe your information. The transponders don't have to be very close to a subject to be able to electronically lift the person's credit card information, including their name and expiration date. It is difficult to determine what percentage of fraud is being committed using this method of theft. However, in order to not be a potential victim you may want to look at putting your credit cards into a protective sleeve like those offered by Identity Stronghold. You should also be aware that as of October 2006, all US passports have RFID transponders embedded in them. While these chips are encrypted and more sophisticated, they can still be scanned and decoded. So placing them in a protective sleeve is also highly recommended.

All Individual Financial Data Records

In 2010, with the passage of the Dodd-Frank Wall Street Reform and Consumer Protection Act, a supposedly "independent agency" was created called The Bureau of Consumer Financial Protection (CFPB). The stated purpose of this agency was to protect the consumer in the financial sector. Ah yes, if life were so simple. Instead it has been discovered through a freedom of information request by Judicial Watch that this agency has spent upwards of $8 million contracting with credit agencies and accounting firms to obtain financial transaction data on American citizens.[14] One contract with Experian is an "indefinite delivery, indefinite quantity" contract that tracks daily consumer habits! I'm sure there is a good reason for this, but at the moment I can't come up with one, can you?

Currency Tracking

Beyond bank reporting, you might be interested to know that, back in 2005, the European Central Bank began working towards embedding radio frequency identification tags into the very fibers of euro bank notes. In 2009, the chip-less RFID, radio-frequency identification tag was being discussed for use in the Australian polymer banknotes as a means for security against counterfeiting. Since that time, many other countries, including Canada, have adopted the use of polymer notes. In addition, the Bank of Japan, as well as Saudi Arabia, has also begun the process of using RFID technology in their currency.

So what does this mean exactly? Well, in short, this means that each and every bill in your pocket could retain a point-to-point history each time the note is scanned. It is not hard to imagine a future where any and all paper documents are registered and tracked from one owner to the next.

Another new method of RFID technology that has recently been developed is known as Laser Enabled Advanced Packaging (LEAP). It has the capability of embedding a traceable chip on paper using a carbon nanotube-infused ink.

Airport Tracking

Attention in the terminal: Your bags aren't the only thing being tracked!

In 2006, CNET News published an article touting an RFID technology called OpTag, concerning its usage in airports. Passengers would be issued RFID-tagged tickets that would allow their movements to be tracked within the airport.[15]

The article stated, "The OpTag system will enable the immediate location of checked-in passengers who are either missing or late, and thus reduce passenger-induced delays and speed up aircraft turn around. The system could also form an essential component of airline passenger identification and threat assessment systems through the automated identification of suspicious passenger movements or through the closer monitoring of individuals considered to pose a risk to secure operations."

**If you want to learn about all the uses of RFID chips, then one of the best sources is: http://www.rfidjournal. com/. What you find will amaze you!

57

CHAPTER FOUR

Glimpse Into The Future

If you want a small peek at what the future technology will bring you can go to the website http://www.afcea.org and look under the Department tab and click the link for Contract Awards. You can then read the brief descriptions of what our government is spending YOUR dollars for. I can guarantee you that you will be surprised at what you will find.

Smart Television

In November of 2013, a United Kingdom technology consultant by the name of Jason Huntley accidentally discovered a menu option on his new LG television, which by default was switched on, allowing the TV to collect information on his viewing habits and then transmit this data back to LG servers.[16] This also included the additional information concerning any DVD content that was connected to his television at the time.

This revelation as to the capability of current technology should not be taken lightly. Just think about this particular intrusion for a moment. Let's say a couple is watching television and, for whatever reason, they get into an argument. All of a sudden on television an advertisement for a relationship counselor appears. Don't be surprised!

The Smart Grid

The electrical grid system of today is based off one-hundred-year-old technology from the 1890s. The customer and utility relationship is one of the customer turning on a switch to receive the power they need when they need it. This relationship is slowly changing into a system known as the smart grid.

Soon every home in America will not only receive electricity, but also be able to transmit data about appliances installed within the home that are controlled by an energy management system. This will give customers a better idea about their own energy usage and ways to reduce their consumption. A question, however, that is currently being discussed is who owns the data that is generated and how will or could that be used?

Solar Flares or EMP

If you search the Internet you will read that, in 1859, a solar storm called the Carrington Event damaged and destroyed telegraphic lines in the United States. In 1989, in Quebec solar storms were blamed for a power grid failure that shut down electricity for nine hours.

One writer described the science behind the above situations: "In a perfect world, direct observations of the sun would translate into detailed alerts describing what the magnetic field will look like when it reaches Earth, where and when the storm will strike, and which grid components will be at most risk. That information would give grid operators several days to prepare. *Today's forecasts offer only about 30 to 45 minutes of lead time."*[17]

So, if you were told you had only thirty minutes to prepare for a disaster that is going to happen, what would your response be? The reality is the government is not likely to warn you of this event because they would not want to create mass panic! You honestly don't hear much in the mainstream media about the threat of solar flares or the potential for an electromagnetic pulse or EMP attack. You won't hear about it, because the media has done an excellent job at suppressing the truth from the general public.

Concerns were raised by a recent Lloyds of London report that stated that the United States electrical grid was extremely vulnerable – so much so that areas like Washington, D.C. and New York, if affected, could be without electrical power for up to two years! A recent congressional EMP commission report also stated, "Contemporary U.S. society is not structured, nor does it have the means, to provide for the needs of nearly 300 million Americans without electricity." In question are approximately three hundred huge electric transformers that needed to be protected from any surge created by either type of event.[18]

In November of 2013, a joint drill called GridExII was conducted in the United States, Canada and Mexico. This involved thousands of utility works, numerous governmental agencies, including the FBI, as well as hundreds of private businesses with a stated goal – "…how governments would react as the loss of the grid crippled the supply chain for everyday necessities." So in essence this exercise is measuring the outcomes of a S.H.T.F. (Shit Hits The Fan) scenario to see what happens.[19]

The United States power grid is NOT fully secured at this point. On April 16, 2013, a major substation owned by the Pacific Power and Gas Company was attacked by gunfire. Fortunately, large scale blackouts were avoided, but the incident still exposed an ugly truth concerning the physical security of our electric grid facilities. It took almost a year since the event occurred for action to be taken on March 7, 2014, by the Federal Energy Regulatory Commission (FERC), which in turn directed the North American Electric Reliability Corporation (NERC) to submit specific physical security reliability standards to (FERC) to address this issue. These standards would then be used by the owners and operators of bulk power systems to address the vulnerably that had been exposed.

On March 12, 2014, Rebecca Smith of the *Wall Street Journal* published an article stating that you could cause a nationwide blackout by disabling nine critical substations out of the 55,000 that are in the United States. A response was given by the former (FERC) chairman Jon Wellinghoff where he stated: "There are probably less than 100 critical high voltage substations on our grid in this country that need to be protected from a physical attack. It is neither a monumental task, nor is it an inordinate sum of money that would be required to do so."[20]

In other words, this is government speak for "move along, nothing to see!" This leaves one to consider an alternative – how you would or could survive long term without electricity. Honestly, this scenario is one that would take more dedicated study and space than is available for this book. Regardless, you need to know about the potential threat and not be ignorant of the facts.

Cyber Attack Threat

If an electromagnetic pulse via a manmade nuclear device or a solar flare from the sun were not enough to worry about, we also have a real and definite threat from cyberspace. Unlike the financial sector, electric utilities are having to fast track their ability to lock down and secure the grid before an attack occurs. The lists of enemies of the United States are numerous: rogue nations and criminal syndicates to so called "hacktivists." All the above have some capability to launch an attack against our critical infrastructure. In recent articles in *Computer World* and a prominent national defense magazine, details are offered about infrastructure attacks that have increased steadily in the past decade.

Below is a list of the events that took place in 2012:

"Shamoon malware: A destructive Trojan horse, which steals data and then wipes files, is allegedly used in an attack that disabled thousands of computers at Saudi Aramco, the national oil company of Saudi Arabia."

"Flame: This highly sophisticated malware is believed to be responsible for data loss incidents at Iran's oil ministry. It was allegedly developed by the U.S. and Israeli governments to collect intelligence about Iran's computer networks that would facilitate future cyber-attacks on computers used in that country's nuclear fuel enrichment program."

"Cyberattacks on natural gas pipeline companies: The Industrial Control Systems Cyber Emergency Response Team (ICS-CERT), which is part of the U.S. Department of Homeland Security, issues an alert to warn of ongoing cyberattacks against the computer networks of U.S. natural gas pipeline companies. The ICS-CERT alert states that the campaign involves narrowly focused spear-phishing scams targeting employees of the pipeline companies."

"Attacks on utilities systems: ICS-CERT issues an alert advising utilities to monitor Internet-facing control systems for activity by hackers attempting to gain remote access to control systems through brute force authentication attacks. The attackers attempted to obtain a user's log-on credentials by guessing usernames and passwords."

"DDoS attacks on U.S. banks: The U.S. accuses Iran of staging a wave of denial-of-service attacks against U.S. financial institutions. In a *New York Times* article, Defense Secretary Leon Panetta warns of potential for a 'cyber Pearl Harbor' against critical infrastructure and calls for new protection standards."[21]

Money Talks – The Secret!

For some people the phrase "money talks" might have a different meaning, but you, the reader, should know the real truth. You might be able to hide money from your spouse, but don't think you can hide money from the government for very long.

You might consider the money you have deposited in a bank yours, but in reality when you deposit money in a bank you are actually treated by law as an *unsecure creditor.*

Sure the bank "owes" you the money, but it is not YOUR money anymore![22]

It is also worth noting that if you withdraw or transfer certain dollar thresholds of YOUR MONEY it will likely trigger a Currency Transaction Report (CTR) or possibly a Suspicious Activity Report (SAR). I know you might think the money is yours to do whatever you want with, but that honestly is not the case as far as the government is concerned.

Currency Transaction Report

"A bank must file a Currency Transaction Report (CTR) (Fin CEN Form 104) for each transaction in currency (deposit, withdrawal, exchange, or other payment or transfer) of more than $10,000 by, through, or to the bank. Certain types of currency transactions need not be reported, such as those involving 'exempt persons,' a group which can include retail or commercial customers meeting specific criteria for exemption."[23]

Suspicious Activity Reporting Requirements

"Certain money service businesses – businesses that provide money transfers or currency dealing or exchange; or businesses that issue, sell, or redeem money orders or traveler's checks – must report suspicious activity involving any transaction or pattern of transactions at or above a certain amount: $2,000 or more; $5,000 or more for issuers reviewing clearance records."[24]

In the United States we have the FDIC, or the Federal Deposit Insurance Corporation, which began back in 1934 to calm the public fears of banks going into bankruptcy and leaving the depositors empty handed. Currently deposits are protected up to $250,000, but this is all predicated on the assumption that there are no massive bank failures nationwide and that the FDIC will have enough money in reserves.

The dirty little secret no one wants to openly and honestly discuss is that the FDIC insures trillions of dollars in deposits with an insurance deposit fund of only billions in reserve. To put things into perspective, you have to venture online and look closely on the www.fdic.gov website and click to look at the latest balance sheet. In 2014, the most current information shown was for 2012, which seems odd in and of itself. Now look specifically at the line titled "Fund as a Percentage of Insured Deposits (reserve ratio)," and you will see the figure for 2012 at .35%.[25]

Safety Deposit Bank Boxes

While it might seem like a relic of the past, millions of people still rent safety deposit boxes annually. However, few, if any, take the time to ask about the operating procedures for securing access, and fewer still ever really read the rental agreement contract. Both are important aspects for you to be familiar with before signing the dotted line. Also, it is important to understand your own state laws that govern access to your box. Many people choose to rent safety deposit boxes jointly and place in these boxes important papers like their original birth certificate, marriage certificate and insurance policies, as well as information on investments or titles to vehicles.

However, you need to be careful not to place items in a safety deposit box that you might need in an emergency – such as a medical directive, power of attorney or an item like a passport. Remember that banks are not open twenty-four hours and are closed on holidays, and in the event of a national emergency it will be unlikely that you will have access to your safety deposit box.

It should also be noted that cash in a safety box is NOT insured by the FDIC, and while banks do have great security, the contents of your safety deposit box are NOT insured by the bank. In order for the contents to be insured you have to purchase your own renter's insurance policy.

Further, you might be interested to know that, in the Spring of 1997 the FDIC Consumer News released a short question-and-answer article that has been posted online specifically addressing the question of who – other than yourself – has the right to gain access to your rented safety deposit box. Moreover, does law enforcement have the ability and/or right to access an individual's safety deposit box without his or her knowledge or permission?

The FDIC article posted this response:

"Mark Mellon, an attorney with the FDIC in Washington, says that if a local, state or federal law enforcement agency persuades the appropriate court that there's 'reasonable cause' to suspect you're hiding something illegal in your box (guns, drugs, explosives, stolen cash or money obtained illegally), 'it can obtain a court order, force the box open and seize the contents.' But what about non-criminal matters, such as a dispute with the Internal Revenue Service, a company or other people over money they say you owe? McGuinn of Safe Deposit Specialists says the IRS can 'freeze' your assets (effectively placing a hold on your bank accounts and safety deposit box) until the dispute is resolved. Private parties also can freeze your assets, but doing so involves going before a judge and proving that there's a legitimate dispute over a debt."[26]

It is also important to note that in most states when the safety deposit box renter dies the box is sealed until the contents can be inventoried for estate tax purposes.

So there you have the facts! Now it is up to you to decide what, if anything, you should keep in a safety deposit box.

Personal Identifiers

Your current social security number is much like the printed barcode. Both are, for the most part, becoming obsolete methods for tracking you and your information. Biometrics have become the key to the future of tracking.

"A biometric or biometric identifier is an objective measurement of a physical characteristic of an individual which, when captured in a database, can be used to verify the identity or check against other entries in the database. The best known biometric is the fingerprint, but others include facial recognition and iris scans."

"In the Enhanced Border Security and Visa Entry Reform Act of 2002, the U.S. Congress mandated the use of biometrics in U.S. visas. This law requires that embassies and consulates abroad must issue, to international visitors, only machine-readable, tamper-resistant visas and other travel and entry documents that use biometric identifiers. Additionally, the Homeland

Security Council decided that the U.S. standard for biometric screening is ten fingerprint scans collected at all U.S. embassies for visa applicants seeking to come to the United States."

"A visa applicant who refuses to be fingerprint-ed would have his or her visa application denied on the basis that it is incomplete. However, an applicant who then later decided to provide fin-gerprints would have his or her visa application re-considered without prejudice."

"Biometrics is a key capability that can identify the enemy, denying him the anonymity he needs to hide and strike at will. The ability to identify and verify individuals is also critical to ensure secure and expeditious business functions. As these biometrics capabilities are applied through various tactics, techniques and processes, they enable a wide range of possible missions, from military operations to business functions that protect national interests."[27]

Facial Recognition

According to www.Privacysos.org, "The federal gov-ernment appears to have already laid the groundwork for the face recognition revolution at our friendly motor vehicle registration departments. Thanks to federal grant programs from the Department of Transportation, at least 35 states have active face recognition programs at their registries of motor vehicles. The states say they use the software to detect fraud and abuse, for example

YOUR PRIVACY AND SECURITY

to catch someone applying for a driver's license under a false name when they already have an ID under their real name. But numerous states are increasingly using the face recognition programs for law enforcement purposes, too. And a new FBI program, disclosed to the public in documents submitted to the Senate Judiciary Committee during the July 2012 hearing on face recognition, makes good use of that federally-funded face recognition technology at motor vehicle registries nationwide for purposes quite apart from fraud detection."[28]

"The FBI's Science and Technology Branch created the BCOE - Biometric Center of Excellence – a one-stop shop for biometric collaboration and expertise – to strengthen our ability to combat crime and terrorism with state-of-the-art biometrics technology. The BCOE, which was established to help meet the challenges and opportunities that the widespread use of biometrics represents, is the FBI's program for advancing the use of new and enhanced biometric capabilities. The BCOE is a collaborative initiative of the Laboratory Division, the Operational Technology Division, the Criminal Justice Information Services Division, and the Special Technologies and Applications Office. Together, scientists, technicians, and biometrics experts are advancing the BCOE's mission to 'foster collaboration, improve information sharing, and advance the adoption of optimal biometric and identity management solutions within the FBI and across the law enforcement and national security communities.'

"Protecting the privacy of individuals also plays an important role in our work. The BCOE is committed to the protection of individual privacy rights and civil liberties. Privacy will be treated as an essential component in the planning and implementation of all BCOE-sponsored initiatives."[29]

The question we have to ask is this: How exactly is the BCOE protecting my privacy?

Further it should be noted that the FBI is in the process of creating a new biometrics database called the Next Generation Identification (NGI). This program, when fully implemented, will ultimately be a database of ALL Americans!

Automated License Plate Readers

The first automatic license number plate recognition (ANPR) technology was invented back in 1976 in the U.K. Since then we have seen this technology used in the United States for various purposes, including identifying those who have a suspended license, or do not have the proper insurance, and locating stolen vehicles.

In 2012, Microsoft announced that the NYPD was implementing their Domain Awareness System (DAS), a sophisticated software program that, among other things, links real-time camera imaging and license plate monitoring. The cameras can also be used for radiation detection. The video captured would normally be retained for thirty days unless archived, and the license plate information would be stored for five years. Certain data that was classified as "environmental data" was said to be stored indefinitely.[30]

It is safe to say that technology today allows law enforcement to record the location of your vehicle regardless of where your vehicle is parked. This information is recorded with a time and date stamp and can be kept indefinitely.

The Black Box

For years most people have heard the term "black box" in association with the data recording device on airplanes. What the public does not know is that the same type of device has been in the vehicle you drive for quite some time now. Event data recorders (EDR) have been in vehicles since the early 1990's, and today over ninety-five percent of all vehicles on the road have these devices in place. By 2014, the National Highway Traffic Administration hopes these devices will be a standard feature in all vehicles.[31]

Unlike the devices in airplanes, currently the EDRs only send data to be stored on the car's onboard computer in the event of a crash. The information transmitted includes deployment of the air bag, the speed of the vehicle, and if any activity was detected within the braking system. Also recorded is the force of the crash and seatbelt usage.

While all this information may legally be the owner of the vehicle's property, fourteen states now allow access by third parties, including law enforcement and lawyers interested in a criminal and/or civil lawsuit, by simply serving the owner with a warrant to obtain disclosure. While all this might come as a surprise to some, it should not.

At a recent conference in 2012, Bill Ford, whose great-grandfather founded Ford Motor Company, spoke about "semiautonomous driving technology," which simply means cars that drive themselves. Technology now gives cars the ability to park themselves as well as to be able to maintain safe distances from other vehicles while driving. Car doors can be opened and closed remotely via satellite as well as determine your exact location. So since it is a fact that 90 percent of all accidents are due to human error, it is not hard to imagine a future where vehicles will be just something you travel in versus actually drive.

No Need To Say Hello!

At this very moment, if you own a cell phone and it is turned on, your current location has been identified. Part of what makes this possible is the SIM card, otherwise known as the Subscriber Identity Module card. This little portable memory chip was inserted into your phone when you purchased it. It identifies your cellular phone with "you" as the subscriber to your specific network. The SIM card also functions as a mini computer that operates various applications on your phone, as well as allowing the chip to store specific user data that includes your phone contact information and your text messages.

Law enforcement agencies further can track individuals with cell phones using one of two different methods. First, they can request specific cell phone tower information, often referred to as "tower dumps," for a certain time period. These reports give information identifying all cell phones that were turned on and their respective location and any activity that might have occurred. Secondly, a roving bug device called the "stingray" can be deployed. This device, when activated, mimics a cell phone tower, allowing it to connect to nearby cell phones in order to pinpoint a specific phone location and gather information – all without your consent or knowledge. Currently at least twenty-five police departments are known to have a stingray device, to the tune of around $400,000.[32]

Writer Susanne Posel recently wrote an article entitled: *How Your Cell Phone Makes Spying Easier for the Government and Police*. Her article, which was published online, states:

"Your wireless company is tracking you with GPS, recording your phone calls and text messages . . . and they are selling the information they collect to other corporations, nations, governments – anyone willing to pay for the data. The U.S. government is one of the wireless corporation's biggest clients. They are collecting yotabytes of data from multiple sources on all American citizens.

"Like a prisoner, your cell phone knows where you go, what you do, when you do it. And so do the U.S. governmental agencies that are interested in this information. CIA hackers are being equipped with spyware that allows them to listen in on your cell phone conversations. Even when your phone is turned off it can be remotely controlled, record information, take pictures, and send this information to the CIA, DHS, NSA, or whoever is controlling your phone."[33]

Knowing all this makes you feel all warm and fuzzy inside, doesn't it? With a simple court order, or not, you can be tracked down faster than you can order a pizza! This brings a whole new meaning to the catch phrase: "Can you hear me now?"

Become AWARE!

OK, the government knows everything there is to know about me, so what? I'm not doing anything wrong or illegal, so why should I care?

These are very good questions! For a moment let's set aside documents like the Constitution or Bill of Rights. The real answer lies in your level of tolerance of what personal freedom and privacy you are willing to "give away."

At what point do you become uncomfortable? At what point have things gone too far?

Say Cheese!

In today's world of digital cameras and smart phone technology, there is a file produced with each photographic image taken called an EXIF file. This is short for an Exchangeable Image File. While most of the information is benign, like the shutter speed or knowing if a flash was used, there is one valuable piece of information this file might contain that could greatly affect your personal safety, and that is the GPS location of where the picture was taken. Think about this for a moment. Is this the ultimate life hack?

John McAfee, the nation's famous anti-virus programmer and creator, might think so. In 2012, while on the run evading authorities, he had given an interview to a magazine that published a picture along with the story. The picture had been taken using the iPhone 4S smart phone and had embedded the GPS coordinates of McAfee's location. He was captured two days later. The best thing to do to protect yourself is to make sure this feature is disabled on your smart phones and digital cameras in the first place.

Sometimes, however, being found can be a good thing, especially when it comes to making sure services like the local police or sheriff's office, or the fire department and rescue squad can find your location. Most cities and counties have an address ordinance that will outline not only the placement, but also the size of the posted street address. This ordinance also will likely govern all road and private access names. To that end, you need to make sure your home has your house numbers displayed properly in case of an emergency.

Whatever the case, you need to be aware of the re-sponse time, or lack thereof, in the case of any emer-gency. You cannot expect law enforcement or any other government agency or service to be available in times of mass crisis. Realistically, you need to prepare for the worst-case scenario. If this scenario never happens then that is a bonus. If it does, you will be ready to respond.

Special Delivery

You might be wondering, what could be next after reading all the above? Well, this news flash comes through the rain, sleet and snow. The Postal Service uses a computer program called the Mail Isolation Control and Tracking (MICT) program. This program photographs and retains an image of the front and back of EVERY piece of mail sorted![34]

So that super-secret order you made that came in that plain brown envelope is not so super-secret anymore, is it? Oops!

Tracking People, Pets or Vehicles

Hooray! You don't have to worry about losing your dog anymore. Also, you can keep tabs on where your kids or spouse are without even asking! Plus you will know how fast they were driving when they got there. All this is done via GPS technology through a consumer product known as the Pocket Finder. Depending on what you want to track, the product varies in size. One rechargeable device is as small as a cookie and weighs only 1.4 ounces. Each device requires an additional fee allowing you to monitor movements. Again, this is the same technology found in your cell phone, but this is geared toward a consumer market. If you carry a smart phone you don't even need any other outside device because, you guessed it, they make an app for that. One of the most popular is called Life 360.

Making A Simple Photocopy

In April of 2010, CBS News did a report exposing the fact that most photocopiers manufactured since 2002 have built-in hard drives.[35] These hard drives are capable of storing the data for every image that was placed in the copier to be faxed or copied. When copying machines are disposed of, many are sent to be reconditioned and sold overseas. It is anyone's guess as to where the data stored goes from there.

Back in 2008, Sharp Computers did a survey and found that 60 percent of consumers knew nothing about photocopy machines having hard drives and the risks involved. While some newer machines offer options that might include the data being erased off the hard drive after the scan is complete, this option comes with an expensive price tag.

Unfortunately, this is yet another risk of which most people are unaware. Think for a moment about hospitals and doctors' offices that lease expensive photocopy machines and where these machines might end up one day – with all sorts of confidential medical information potentially exposed.

CHAPTER FIVE

Your Life

You might not have a computer or even know how to use one, but information about you has nonetheless been stored and placed online. Beyond any covert means to access information, ordinary individuals can determine a lot about you and where you live by accessing the Internet. One website that is worth investigating to give you an understanding of the amount of public data that is exposed can be found at the Public Records Free Directory - http://publicrecords.onlinesearches.com/.

With various websites, those up to no good can identify lucrative properties to break into and also find a list of the people who reside at your location. The data sometimes can include a phone number, as well as the ages of the individuals living at that address. Having your phone number is a handy tool that allows an individual to call your home while they are waiting outside to make sure no one answers before they break in.

If you have not already done so, I suggest you go online and type in your name as well as do additional searches using your home address and phone number.

Try www.pipl.com as a quick starting point. Next, go to http://www.spokeo.com/, http://www.cvgadget. com/ and finally http://www.zabasearch.com/. Use various search engines you normally use and try various combinations of your name, address and phone number to see what you can find. It should be no surprise, but http://www.ancestry.com can also be an invaluable resource.

What you are seeing online is merely very basic surface data that is easily obtained and, therefore, freely displayed. But what about the other information that has been collected and is considered more valuable? Are you comfortable with everyone knowing your personal habits, buying patterns or even your health status? Most people have not really heard of the term "data brokers," but we likely have had some interaction with these companies: Equifax, Experian, TransUnion or Dunn and Bradstreet.

A data broker, simply put, is an individual or company that gathers all the available information on a person or group of people from public and private sources. They, in turn, sell this information to individuals or organizations for their purposes.

We have all heard the axiom that "information is power," and apparently that power is sellable as well and can be used for both good and evil. It is important that you, the reader, fully understand the magnitude of the amount of information that is floating around in cyberspace and on private corporate computer servers.

One such company you have probably never heard of is a company known as Acxiom Corp. Acxiom actually started in 1969 under the name Demographics Inc., and at that time they utilized rather basic information via phone books and voter records to start their database. Today, forty-plus years later, they have records on over 190 million people and over 126 million households. They operate a staggering 23,000 servers that collect 50 trillion data transactions annually![36]

Another data mining company that is known primarily as a credit-reporting agency is Experian. They have a consumer list of 210 million consumers that represent 110 million households. They also have a list of more than 14 million businesses. With these lists they can help build either a direct mail or e-mail campaign for the user. Additional lists include new parents, new homeowners, new movers and high-income new movers. People that have a mortgage, rent, or invest are all targets. If you are a health or sports enthusiast or are interested in environmental causes you are also on a list.[37]

To further drive this point home, you should be aware of a recent Forbes magazine article dated February 2012 that was titled: "How Target Figured Out A Teen Girl Was Pregnant Before Her Father Did."[38] The article examines the data mining practices of the retail giant Target. Every individual customer is assigned a guest ID number that is linked to his or her credit card information and tracks all your purchases and any other information they have been able to collect on you. By taking information from ladies that have signed up on Target's baby registry, as well as looking at the person's buying pattern based on approximately twenty-five products, their own in-house statistician, Andrew Pole, can predict with an 87 percent accuracy level the "due date" of the expectant mother. With this prediction, a flood of coupons would come to the mom-to-be in hopes that she would shop for her baby at Target.

None of this is illegal, but again I will ask you to ponder the question I asked earlier: At what point do you consider this a threat? If this is not a "threat," do you think this is an invasion of your privacy that should be protected?

Can you Opt-Out?

Simply put, if you use a phone, a credit card, the Internet or a whole host of other interactions in the course of living your life, you will be tracked for purposes beyond your control. So the answer is unfortunately NO, not entirely.

The best explanation of the process is to understand that as a consumer you are constantly generating information based on your purchases and payment history. You could place a request to opt-out of a database on Monday and some information may be erased, but the holders of the information are under NO obligation to actually comply. Plus, additional information will flow into the database on a continual basis, so more than likely your information will again find its way back into the database. Once the cat is out of the bag you can't put it back in and expect it to stay put!

What You CAN And SHOULD Do!

There are certain steps you should take to actively manage what is known about you and how it is used. Again, you may not be able to totally control how data is used, but you can be aware of its existence and what it discloses, as well as attempt to limit your electronic footprint.

Telephone Risks

The telephone is a wonderful communication device that allows you the ease of keeping in contact with both family and friends; however, in today's world this common device in many ways has become a nuisance, with the onslaught of annoying telemarketing and survey calls that rarely offer something you want or need. One key point that can't be stressed enough, especially to the very young and the elderly, is that you should never disclose any information, no matter how trivial it might seem, to a total stranger. If you find yourself being asked a question you don't want to answer, simply say you are busy and will call them back later. Also this gives you time to think and, if need be, to verify the person calling is legitimate. If someone calls asking to speak to a man in your house, do not disclose anything that might suggest you are living alone or that there is not a male presence at that location. If you have children it is important to teach them what to say and what not to say.

National Do Not Call Registry – Telemarketing Calls

It is more than a little annoying to have your phone ring and you answer only to hear a recording from a company that you never heard of trying to sell you something. What is worse are the survey calls, or people that you might have ordered something from in the past calling to tell you about a special on something they are selling that you have absolutely no interest in. Harassment via the phone line has become an epidemic for consumers who just want to be left alone. The insanity is that the government has the capability to gather all the phone numbers and conversations that take place, but have yet to shut down all the illegal and annoying telemarketers that harass people daily.

The only solution at this point is to register with the Do Not Call Registry by calling toll-free 888-382-1222 to add the number to the opt-out list. You can also go online to www.donotcall.gov for more information.

BEWARE: Never give ANY personal information to someone who calls you on the phone that you do not know! Do NOT take surveys over the phone or in person. The risks far outweigh any benefits you may receive.

Opting Out - Prescreened Offers of Credit and Insurance

There are four consumer credit reporting compa-nies today – Equifax, Experian, TransUnion and In-novis. Under the Fair Credit Reporting Act (FCRA), they are allowed to provide your credit file information to companies making firm offers of credit or insurance that you have NOT requested. These preapproved or prescreened offers can be quite annoying, and they can pose a serious threat to you by way of potential identity theft.

The Fair Credit Reporting Act, however, does provide consumers several options to "opt-out." First you can choose to opt-out of firm offers for credit and insurance for five years, or with a little more effort on your part, you can be placed on a list that will opt out your information permanently.

There is only one Internet website that all four credit agencies have authorized to handle this opt-out process, and that site is www.OptOutPrescreen. com. By going online you can click and send in your information which will automatically place you on the opt-out list for five years. If you wish to opt-out on a permanent basis you will also be required to print and sign a form printed from their website and mail it to them. If you feel uncomfortable doing one or both you can call 888-5-OPT-OUT or 888-567-8688 and start this process over the phone.

Note that you still may receive some offers from companies that do not use information from the credit reporting agencies, but from other sources. Also, your information may have already been provided prior to your request.

Junk Mail – DMA Opt Outs

Receiving junk mail is another sometimes-difficult problem to tackle in the effort to try to decrease your identity footprint. The first place to start is the Direct Mail Association (DMA), https://www.dmachoice.org/. This company operates as a trade group for approximately 3,600 members who represent businesses or non-profits that use direct mail. By registering on their website you can access their tool called DMAchoice™. This tool will allow you to manage catalog, magazine and other mail offers as well as set up a your telephone preference choice. Note that while this is helpful, there is a limitation in that these lists are only used by member organizations, so this alone unfortunately will not necessarily solve all your junk mail problems.

The U.S. Postal Service also recently introduced its own direct mail program called Every Door Direct Mail® or EDDM for short. Basically, this allows any business to do a targeted promotion mailing that is delivered to a specific route location without having to have a mailing list or listing any specific names or addresses on the promotional mail. In typical government fashion, in crafting this program they did not account for people not wishing to get this junk mail, so at the moment there is no real method to opt out.

Financial Institution Privacy Statements

We all receive numerous privacy statements in the mail, but rarely does anyone take the time to read what they say. Why? The answer lies in the title of the March 1, 2012, article from *The Atlantic* entitled: "Reading the Privacy Policies You Encounter in a Year Would Take 76 Work Days."[39]

Beyond the time involved, the legalese in most privacy statements is enough to make anyone's head spin. Many times the privacy notice is posted on the financial institution's website. The specific method to opt out, be it by letter, phone or online, is determined on a case-by-case basis by each institution. So, if you want to do what is necessary to remove yourself from ALL the lists that contain your information, you need to ask for a copy of the privacy notice for EVERYONE with whom you have a business relationship, not just financial institutions, and review each document to find the section on how to opt out.

Credit Freeze

If you are worried about the potential threat of someone trying to open fraudulent accounts to secure credit, then the most effective way to handle this threat is to contact all of the credit bureaus and place a "security freeze" on your account. This denies access to potential creditors or sellers of services because they will not be able to access your credit file. Below is the contact information for the credit agencies:

Experian:
http://www.experian.com/consumer/security_freeze.html
Phone: 888-397-3742

TransUnion:
http://www.transunion.com/personal-credit/credit-disputes/credit-freezes.page
Phone: 800-680-7289

Equifax:
https://help.equifax.com/app/answers/detail/a_
id/158/~/security-freezes
Phone: 888-766-0008

Innovis:
https://www.innovis.com/InnovisWeb/pers_
placeSecurityFreeze.html
Phone: 800-540-2505

Data Broker Opt Outs

As mentioned earlier, data brokers play a huge role in gathering and maintaining databases about who we are, what we purchase and the choices we make daily. Unfortunately, these companies are not under any legal obligation to do anything to limit the use of YOUR private information; you are literally at their mercy!

Most companies offer some method to opt out, but this is not necessarily going to guarantee that your information is totally deleted. Two of the largest data brokers are Acxiom and Lexis Nexis. Below is the information you need to request that your information is removed.

Acxiom:
You can request to opt out by sending an e-mail to optoutus@acxiom.com or by calling 877-774-2094. It is also advisable to go to this page on their web-site to review the information listed: http://www. acxiom.com/8588/consumer-information.

Lexis Nexis:
"Individuals may opt-out of having personal information about themselves made available through KnowX® and Accurint®, in accordance with legal requirements or if permitted by LexisNexis policy."
"Each opt-out request must include documentation substantiating the risk of physical harm or the individual's status as an identity theft victim or as a person otherwise meeting the above criteria. LexisNexis reserves the right to determine in its sole reasonable discretion what documentation meets the above criteria. If your opt-out request is not approved we will promptly inform you about that determination."
The form that you fill out can be found at the following web address: https://www.lexisnexis.com/opt-out-public-facing-products/Default.aspx

FERPA - Family Educational Rights and Privacy Act – Opt Out

School records, for the most part, are protected and can only be released with written consent. However, schools retain the right to "directory information" that may include the person's name as well as permanent address listed, dates of attendance, degree received, etc. If you wish to opt out of the release of that information, you must contact the school and make a request and will likely be required to fill out a form from the institution to restrict the directory information they disclose.

CHAPTER SIX

Online Security

WE Do It To Ourselves!

It is amazing how seemingly private people can be so public when it comes to telling everyone about the inner workings of their lives on Facebook™, Twitter™, Foursquare™ and other social networks.

People disclose all sorts of private information about where they are going, when they get there, what they are doing, and the times they are doing it. All this is ripe for the picking for individuals with ill intentions. You need to be aware that the information disclosed might not only be coming from the actual person, but other family members or their friends that might know you are going on that vacation and share that tidbit of information on their Facebook™ page. According to one article, Facebook™ users upload 2.5 billion images a month! It's no wonder everyone knows everything about our lives.[40]

Surfing Privacy Online

Since it is nearly impossible to use the Internet

and avoid some sort of tracking, the best solution to date is to have as your home page and the starting point of EVERY inquiry a search engine known as www.startpage.com. The following is from the search engine's website:

> "StartPage and its sister search engine Ixquick have, in their 14-year history, never provided a single byte of user data to the US government, or any other government or agency. Not under PRISM, nor under any other program in the US, nor under any program anywhere in the world. We are not like Yahoo, Facebook, Google, Apple, Skype, or the other US companies who got caught up in the web of PRISM surveillance."

> "StartPage does not store any user data. We make this perfectly clear to everyone, including any governmental agencies. We do not record the IP addresses of our users and we don't use tracking cookies, so there is literally no data about you on our servers to access. Since we don't even know who our customers are, we can't share anything with Big Brother. In fact, we've never gotten even a single request from a governmental authority to supply user data in the fourteen years we've been in business."[41]

Finally, if you search the web and constantly find that you are being bombarded by pop-up ads, you can install a free open source program called Ad Block Plus to help prevent those ads from being displayed.

Keeping Secret Passwords Secret

If you are like a lot of people, you are spending more and more time online. This requires you to log in to websites using a user name and password. The list of websites that require you to log in seem endless – Facebook™, eBay™ and Amazon™ are just the beginning. With instant and twenty-four hour access to your accounts, the exposure to risk is tremendous. You might be wondering how easy it is to hack into your account. The amount of time will likely shock you. If your password is five characters or less it could take only a matter of seconds using software that can be downloaded for free!

On www.lifehacker.com, Internet standards expert and blogger John Pozadzides wrote an article that listed ten things that approximately 20 percent of us use in creating our passwords. Those ten things are:

1. Your partner, child, or pet's name, possibly followed by a 0 or 1 (because they're always making you use a number, aren't they?)
2. The last 4 digits of your social security number.
3. 123 or 1234 or 123456.
4. "password"
5. Your city, college, or football team name.
6. Date of birth – yours, your partner's or your child's.
7. "god"
8. "letmein"
9. "money"
10. "love"

Beyond these simple things, he further discloses that we make ourselves vulnerable to hacking when we use the same passwords for multiple accounts because it is easy for us to remember. So, instead of logging into a bank account server that is likely protected against multiple unsuccessful log in attempts with a user name and password, the attacker would pick other website accounts and use computer software, a lot that are free to download, to try all the various combinations.[42]

Passwords obviously need to be both memorable and secure. The password length needs to be at least eight characters. Also you need to use not only lower case letters in creating your password, but upper case as well. You also need to include both symbols and numbers. Finally, try not to use the same password for everything! I know this is asking a lot, but it's not impossible.

Online Shopping

As you browse the web looking for deals, you need to be careful to make sure you are dealing with a reputable online retailer. Make sure you are using the most up-to-date Internet browser, and look for sites that display digital certificates authenticating that the website is a valid site. One well-known independent service is VeriSign, and you also may see a company called Trust-E that shows that the company's privacy statement has been reviewed and that the information you enter should remain secure. If possible, use only one credit card when you make purchases so that you can more easily review the statement. Also, make sure you keep copies of your Internet purchases and print out the confirmation e-mail most sites send after a purchase is made that gives you the order number and information needed in the event you need to contact customer service.

Warranty/Registration Cards

Most experts agree that warranty cards and product registration cards are nothing but marketing ploys to gather data about you the consumer and should be avoided. This information could easily be sold without your consent, and you would likely end up on yet another mailing list you did not intend to be placed on. Many times you will notice that the questions on the card are broad and ask for information that has no bearing on your purchase. The best action to take is to simply keep the warranty card and your original receipt and place them in a folder in a drawer for safekeeping.

Removing Your Online Footprint

Most of us fail to realize that the world is watching, or at least has the potential to watch. In order to control what is known about us, we have to go to the source of this information – ourselves. You have to ask yourself, is the risk worth the exposure? Only you can decide! How much of your life do you want to be on display? How easily do you want others to contact you? Below are a few steps you may want to consider if you are serious about limiting the public information about you that is displayed.

How to close your Facebook account:
http://www.facebook.com/help/224562897555674
How to close your LinkedIn Account:
http://help.linkedin.com/app/answers/detail/a_id/63
How to close your Twitter Account:
http://support.twitter.com/articles/15358-
deactivating-your-account#

Cookies – Not the Kind You Eat

A cookie is a computer-generated text file that is placed on your computer to identify your web activity. This tag basically records the number of times you visited a site and where you went on the site. Some people could care less that advertisers could track your movements, and others feel this is yet another invasion of privacy.

The Network Advertising Initiative (NAI) is a trade group of 90 online advertisers who collect information about you by enabling those pesky electronic cookies that track your choices and movements. While this may be akin to removing one bucket of sand off the beach, they do offer a one-click opt-out system that should protect users from online tracking of their activity from these advertisers. Go to the consumer opt-out button on this page: http://www.networkadvertising. org/managing/opt_out.asp.

Most Internet browsers allow you to change your privacy settings to block certain cookies; however, this sometimes affects how the website is displayed. If you are still concerned then you may want to look at a software program called Ghostery.

"Ghostery is your window into the invisible web – tags, web bugs, pixels and beacons that are included on web pages in order to get an idea of your online behavior. Ghostery tracks over 1,400 trackers and gives you a roll-call of the ad networks, behavioral data providers, web publishers, and other companies interested in your activity." Learn more by going to http://www.ghostery.com/

Spam – Spoof – Phishing

While the above title might remind you of watching a Batman™ TV show with the subtitles, I can assure you the risks online are far from make-believe.

First, let's explore the common, everyday online junk mail known as spam. This uninvited intrusion into your electronic mailbox is both annoying and time consuming, but not a huge threat. Different schools of thought abound, with some telling you to click any opt-out feature provided in these e-mails, whereas others will tell you that this in fact only identifies that your mailbox is real and working and may encourage more unwanted messages to arrive. Beyond using spam filters on your e-mail account, the most effective way to rid yourself of this burden is to limit displaying your e-mail online embedded in any document or listed on any website. Some people choose to create two e-mail accounts and use one for personal communications only, and then use another when making purchases online or responding to organizations that might retain your information to add to a mailing list.

The next set of issues involves a spoof or fake e-mail, or phishing attempt, to gain private information about you that could include your date of birth or a specific account number or password with the ultimate goal of attempting to use this information to commit fraud. These types of e-mails often look very official, using the company logos, and they have web addresses that look like they are coming from a legitimate source. The e-mail also might look like an online confirmation informing you that a 42-inch flat screen TV was just mailed to someone you do not know and you were charged. If you click the link, you will be told to enter in your user name and password. That is when the information will be used to access your account and a charge will be made.

If you get an e-mail and are in doubt, DO NOT CLICK ANY LINK on the message. Instead do an online search and find the company's phone number and call to inquire about the e-mail you received.

Additional Online Protection

If you actively do Internet searches, then your computer needs some form of virus protection. The following is a list of FREE software programs you can search and download to help protect your computer from various threats. They include Microsoft Security Essentials, VIPRE, MalwareBytes Anti-Malware, SuperAntiSpyware, SpyBot Search and Destroy, and ZoneAlarm that offer firewall protection. You may want to look at another program called CCleaner, which is a tool used to delete all temporary files, cookies, and fix minor registry errors.

Wireless Encryption

If you have a home computer system that offers a wireless way to connect, you need to make sure the connection is password secured and protected. Likewise, you need to be aware that free WiFi networks, also known as wireless hotspots that do not require you to log in with a password and are often found at restaurants or in airports, are not secure. The information you type, including passwords or account information, could potentially be intercepted!

There are two basic ways this can occur. One method is that the hacker can turn his computer into a wireless network hotspot at a coffee shop, library, airport, hotel or university and wait for someone to connect. The unsuspecting person is actually connected through the hacker's computer, and all the information entered is intercepted and stored. A virus can be transmitted to download all the information stored on your hard drive.

Another way is to simply intercept the signals your computer transmits as you use an unsecure wireless connection. When you use your computer with a wireless connection you are in fact transmitting a radio wave, and with the right software anyone can tune into that transmission much like you tune a radio to hear a specific radio station.

In short, the solution is not to use unsecured wireless networks or to subscribe to a private WiFi service like http://www.privatewifi.com/ that encrypts everything you send and receive with bank-level security.

Computer and Cell Phone Disposal

It is important when you dispose of your cell phone or computer that you remember to remove all the electronic data that is stored on each device. For phones, this would mean deleting all your call and text information as well as your contact data. You may want to even consider removing the SIM card. For a computer it is more difficult. You can search online for the latest utility wiping programs to remove data from your hard drive. However, if you are still concerned that some data might be recoverable, then your best option is to disassemble the hard drive and remove the drive's platters, place rare earth magnets on the surface, sand the surface, then drill holes and break them apart in little pieces before disposing of them.

Peek-A-Boo – I See You!

If you have a laptop with a built-in webcam or a computer that has a webcam attached, then you need to be aware how easy it is for someone to breach security and view what you are doing without you being aware of it.

How does this happen? You receive an e-mail like a greeting card, or you happen to click your computer mouse to view a random link that turns out not to be just information, but a computer virus that secretly downloads to your computer. The virus then allows your computer to be controlled remotely even when it is in sleep mode. At any time the computer can be switched to view and see whatever is taking place or hear any sounds near your computer.

The solution is to shut your computer off completely, as well as cover the camera with something to block the view.

Computer Theft

You need to have a plan of what you will do in the event your hard drive crashes or your home is broken into and your computer is stolen.

Many people have chosen to use a service like Carbonite: http://www.carbonite.com to back up their computer on a regular basis. Others back up important documents on internal or external hard drives or use a removable thumb drive. Regardless of the method, you should use whatever option or options you feel is right for your situation.

Much like making a habit of locking your doors both during the day and night, you need to make a habit of also remembering to protect the important information you have stored on your computer by creating and maintaining a current back up and keeping this copy in a safe location. In the event of theft, there are several products you many want to look into that can help in the recovery of your computer:

Absolute Software:
http://www.absolute.com/lojackforlaptops/

YOUR PRIVACY AND SECURITY

Laptop Cop:
http://www.laptopcopsoftware.com/

For Mac users the program Hidden
http://hiddenapp.com/ can be used.

Each of the software products mentioned have different features and all come with annual subscription charges. However, using products like these will inevitably give you a much better chance of finding your stolen laptop or home computer than without it.

CHAPTER SEVEN
A Blanket of Security

Most of us feel fairly secure in our home or in our car while driving. We are not on guard, and we don't necessarily have a heightened sense of security all the time. That would be impractical. However, we do need to make sure that we are not so distracted that we become sloppy and fail to take the necessary steps to be secure.

Common sense advice includes keeping your storm door as well as exterior doors locked when at home. If you have an alarm system, make sure you use it.

When you walk into any building – be it at home, in your office or even in your favorite restaurant – in your mind create an exit plan. Simply put, look around and think of the ways you could quickly exit beyond the door you just entered. If you are in a restaurant, make a point of sitting facing the main entrance versus having your back towards the door.

Keep your car doors locked at all times, whether the car is in the driveway or in your garage. Make a habit of locking the door when you get in or out.

As you go about your daily routine, moving from point A to point B, keep your head up and look around before proceeding rather than staring at the ground and trying not to make eye contact with the people around you. If you are going to your car or truck have the keys out and ready to use. Each time you make a transition, be aware of your surroundings.

When driving, have in your mind places to which you could travel quickly in the event you feel threatened. These "zones of safety" could include places like a police station, fire station or hospital. Also think of any businesses in the area with security that are open during the day or night.

Lastly, I'm reminded of a childhood phrase that has stayed with me throughout my life and is a decent mantra to remember as we consider our own personal security: "Look both ways before you cross the street. Use your eyes, use your ears and then use your feet."

Shopping Tips

Women have to remain especially vigilant while making the transitions from point A to B. Your antenna needs to be up as you move from the house to the car or the parking lot to the building. If you go to a convenience store, look to make sure you see the clerk inside before entering the store. Again, if it does not look safe or you see people who appear to be just hanging around, go elsewhere. If you are in a store and are ready to leave and you start to feel uncomfortable, ask for assistance and have a store manager escort you to your vehicle.

Always listen to your instincts and NEVER ignore them. If you see a stranger who makes you feel uncomfortable, don't ignore this. Leave and keep yourself from getting into harm's way. Beware of the "friendly stranger" who offers to help you hold or carry your packages to the car. We have a tendency to want to "be nice" to people and not offend them, but your personal security trumps any hurt feelings an individual might have. Be firm in your response and politely decline any offers for assistance from strangers.

It is important to take into consideration the shoes you are wearing. For some high heels would make it difficult to move fast or run in the event of an emergency. Realize wearing flashy jewelry or carrying a large bulky pocketbook could put you at greater risk. While your expensive designer purse may only contain a few dollars, a tube of lipstick, tissues and a pack of Nabs™, a purse snatcher will think otherwise. It is imperative that women limit what they carry and not be tied to their purse, both literally and figuratively.

There are companies that sell camera bags and purses with straps that are cut resistant. While this might seem like a good idea, there is nothing you have on your person that is worth losing your life over!

At a restaurant, keep your purse either in your lap or on the floor between your feet, not draped around the back of your chair. If someone does snatch your purse, point at the person and yell, "Police, stop him!" to focus the attention on the person committing the crime. If you just say "help" you draw the attention to you.

Store Loyalty Cards – Carrot or Stick?

Most people succumb to signing up for a loyalty card because of the enticement for discounts that are advertised.

If you delve deeper, you will find that to pay for this program stores first raise the retail prices on certain products they plan on discounting so they can show a "savings" when using their loyalty card. The cashier may even circle this amount and proudly state that with your purchase you have saved X dollars, when the truth of the matter is you have not really saved much of anything at all, but simply received the manufacturer's suggested retail price that you would have normally gotten before this charade began.

First and foremost, there are privacy concerns from gathering all this data. Even if you sign up using a bogus name and address, the stores still use your purchase information as a tool to set up a two-tiered pricing structure for those who use the card and those who don't. But also there is something more that you need to know.

Have you ever wondered why the store you have been shopping at all of a sudden discontinued selling the item you purchased? Well, one answer can be found by recognizing that stores seek to identify their most loyal shoppers, because those shoppers are the ones who generate their highest profit. Studies have shown over and over that approximately 75 percent of purchases come from only 30 percent of the customers.

This means that stores are driven to stock the shelves by what those "most loyal customers" purchase, which directly determines the availability of the merchandise they carry.

There is one main consumer group that vehemently opposes the promotion of loyalty card programs and that group's name is CASPIAN, which stands for the Consumers Against Supermarket Privacy Invasion And Numbering.

"CASPIAN was founded in October 1999 to oppose grocery store 'loyalty cards.' Our initial research into supermarket cards and data collection led us to look into the multi-billion dollar 'CRM' or 'Customer Relationship Management' industry that makes its living by collecting and trafficking in people's personal data. We were horrified at what we discovered, and even more concerned at how little the average American knows about this industry that daily invades their privacy."[43]

Your Wallet

In the event your wallet is taken or misplaced, it is imperative that you know in advance the contents of the items missing. Information like PIN numbers, bank account numbers or, worst of all, your social security number should NEVER be carried in your wallet! These open you up to additional threats to your financial security and would add insult to injury.

Most people carry a driver's license and multiple credit cards, but many of us hold onto old receipts, coupons and bits of worthless paper that have found their way into the contents, most of which are not needed and should be properly shredded and destroyed.

You should take the time to go NOW and purchase an inexpensive notebook and write a list of all the cards and account numbers in your wallet, as well the wallet of any other person in your family. Locate the phone number that is usually printed on the back of the card you would need to call to report if a card were lost or stolen.

In this same notebook, you should consider having another section to record other information that you deem important, with the mindset that the notebook will serve as a tool you would use – in the event of a disaster – to help you in the recovery process. Also note, if your home were broken into electronics are some of the first items to be taken, so this is why it is important not to store all your data on a computer exclusively. Few thieves would bother with looking twice at a cheap paper notebook.

You will want to keep this notebook handy, because this should be one of the first items you should grab in case of an emergency and you have to evacuate. Also while you are not in a rush or panic you should consider taking the time to secure a duplicate driver's license. Many times this can be done online and takes just a few minutes. Your license will arrive in the mail within a few weeks. These are proactive steps to take now that will save some headaches later in the event that you unfortunately have to report the loss.

Store your notebook in a secure place in a heavy-duty sealable plastic bag, preferably one that is water resistant.

If you have a passport and/or birth certificate place these in your bag also. If you have a cell phone, place in your phone contacts the numbers found on the back of your credit cards and also add the phone number to the credit reporting agencies in the event you need to report to them that your cards have been lost or stolen. You would likely need to have at the minimum a credit watch or possibly a credit freeze placed on your account: Experian: 888-397-3742, TransUnion: 800-680-7289, Equifax: 888-766-0008 and Innovis: 800-540-2505.

DO consider creating and carrying an ICE Card, i.e. In Case of Emergency. You may wish to laminate the card. The card should contain your name, address and year of birth. List at least one, if not two, contact names with primary and alternate phone numbers. List any current medical conditions and allergies and the name and phone number, including area code, of your primary care doctor. You can also find free templates for an ICE Card you can carry by simply going to any search engine and typing in the words ICE Card.

Your emergency contact numbers should also be added to your cell phone and listed under the contact name ICE. If you have a Smart phone you can also find an ICE App.

Cash and Carry

Closely examine everything you carry on your person and ask yourself if you really need to carry each item. If you lose any of these things, what risk does this pose?

Again, NEVER carry your social security card! This number provides access to critical areas of your life, and you are rarely asked to produce the original form, so you should commit this number to memory. Don't cheat and write it on another paper either!

Limit the cash you carry, and if you are going out-of-town for an extended period of time or on vacation consider travelers checks as an alternative, or simply use your credit card.

ATM/Debit Card Security

As mentioned earlier, it is vital that you protect your PIN number and not have this number written down in your wallet. When you are approaching an ATM machine, slow down and look carefully around you to see if anyone is nearby. If you can, bring a friend along so they can keep a lookout for you as you make your transaction.

Be aware of a technique called "shoulder surfing," whereby a person stands close by casually looking over your shoulder. This can happen easily in places you might tend to ignore, like at the grocery store or post office. Don't feel uncomfortable covering the keypad with one hand while you enter your PIN number with the other. If you are using a drive up ATM, again take your time to look and make sure no one is around, and if they are move on to another machine. A large percentage of robberies at ATMs occur after 7 p.m., so if at all possible do your transactions earlier in the day. Do not give your PIN number out to anyone, especially if you are approached and the person identifies himself as someone from the bank, as this is likely a scam.

The Boogie Man

As children, we were all taught that the unknown was something we should fear. As adults we still carry this fear, and some of us have a deep-seated feeling that someone is out to get us around every corner. This would be a good time to dispel this common myth and break the bonds of inadequacy so that we can start to feel secure in our own personal abilities.

Having a healthy respect for the unknown is warranted, yet there is a fine line between this self-awareness and paranoia. Try, if you can, to adjust your thinking to being the one in the driver's seat versus a lonely passenger. Every time you wake up in the morning you should not fear something bad happening to you; instead, be confident living another day.

Our Sixth Sense or Gut Feelings

We have all been blessed in some form or another with an inborn instinct for self-preservation. This might mean different things to different people, but most can recall a moment when they knew it was not in their best interest to proceed in a certain direction or go to a particular location.

You need to heed those inner warnings! No possession is worth your life, and no everyday task is worth the risk. If you feel uncomfortable in a parking lot, then don't get out of the car and leave. If you are in a store and feel uneasy going to the car, then ask for help from someone in the store to go with you. Retreating for safety is a good option no matter the circumstances!

Curious George

When bad things happen, we are in many ways drawn to the attention it brings. We "rubber neck" at car crashes looking to see what happened, and in many instances we become more of a danger to others due to our distractions. Likewise, if we find ourselves in a crowd and hear lots of shouting, we want to see what is happening versus taking the more common sense approach and moving away from potential danger. It is hard to break all these natural tendencies that we have, but it would serve us well to recognize these as what they are – a threat to our personal security – and try to adjust our thinking as we move forward.

Finally, if you ever find yourself arriving home and you see your front door wide open or see a broken window DO NOT go inside to investigate. Quickly move away to a safe distance, and if you have a cell phone call the police. If not go to a neighbor's home and ask them to call the police. The person or persons could still be inside, and you need to let law enforcement who are trained to handle these situations go inside to make sure everything is secure.

Trash or Treasure

The old saying is true: "One man's trash is another man's treasure," but there is more to this cliché than you might imagine. Every week, most of us place all sorts of free information about ourselves on the curb. Of course, if you have used any type of store discount card, a long list of your preferences have already been recorded and are known by someone. Thankfully, however, our lives are boring and mundane, and we do not have paparazzi outside taking pictures of us in less-than-flattering poses as we make our way outside to pick up a morning paper or get in our car.

Regardless, you need to ask yourself what would happen if someone other than the trash collector picked up your trash and sorted through it and published the contents on the front page of your local newspaper. Would they find anything you would not want to be made public knowledge?

You might be surprised to know that an article in *Police Chief Magazine* was entitled: *"The Use of Garbage to Establish Probable Cause for Granting Valid Search Warrants."* In this article it stated the following: "There is no reasonable expectation of privacy for trash after it has been placed out for pickup."[44] That is right – what you throw away is open for public scrutiny.

Likewise, I am reminded of a case involving a murder suspect. DNA evidence was needed to connect him to the crime. Detectives followed the suspect, who was a heavy smoker, and waited until he tossed a cigarette butt on the ground. The butt was retrieved and DNA tests done and the suspect was charged and eventually convicted. Another case involved a suspect being asked, in the presence of officers posing as people conducting a survey, to complete and seal the survey in an envelope. Once the suspect licked and sealed the envelope, the DNA evidence was then processed, and again a conviction eventually occurred.

**Note: Some have called trash placed by the curb "burglar bait." Nothing screams louder than having the discarded cardboard box to your new 60-inch flat screen TV on the curb for recycling. Think twice before placing this at the curb in front of your house. If you have no other way to dispose of it, think about at least tearing down the box and placing it in a black garbage bag.

Shred Fest

Think about all the information you have around your house that tells the silent story about you: labels on prescription medicines, credit card receipts, a phone bill listing who you called, as well as the piles of catalogs that have your name and address and customer ID numbers not just printed on the outside of the catalog, but many times also printed on the inside order form.

We all are guilty of casually throwing away documents that have personal information on them, items that could put our identity at risk. Beyond simply tearing up a piece of paper a few times, what should you do to protect yourself?

In many cities they have annual events where you can bring old documents you no longer need to shred free of charge. You might want to check with your local city or county to see if they offer such a service. But most of us don't want to hold on to every piece of paper we get for that long. So you should seriously consider purchasing your own shredder.

There are basically three types of shredders. The first and least effective is a ribbon shredder. Government agencies and others have been known to re-assemble material that passes through this type of shedder in as little as one hour. The second type of shredder is a crisscross or diamond cut shredder. These shreds are more difficult to reconstruct. However, information that passes through this type of shredder can be pieced back together in about eight hours. Finally, the best shredder to buy is a micro cut shredder that cuts paper into confetti. Almost all government agencies use this type of shredder, and it is considered the safest for protecting information.

Another protective measure that is not as secure as shredding, but better than doing nothing, uses a self-inking stamp. When pressed over the information, an ink pattern blocks the writing to leave it undistinguishable. You can go online and search for "ID Blocking Stamp" to see the various products offered.

Stop Check and Document Fraud

Today people are writing fewer and fewer checks and are moving more towards paying their bills online. As far as identity theft is concerned, this is probably a good thing, because when a check is written it passes through numerous hands, all which are potential points of exposure to fraud.

Everyone knows you should guard your checkbook,

but this also includes your deposit slips. A crook could just as easily have a bogus check to deposit and withdraw money on the cash received line as part of their scam. Make sure ONLY your name and address are listed on your checks and deposit slips and not your driver's license number.

To help stop any possible check fraud via "check washing" or document fraud you should consider a simple $2 solution. Buy the Uni-ball™ 207 Gel Pen! This pen features the Uni Super Ink™ that permanently binds itself to the paper you write on and cannot be washed off or removed, period. This is one of the best pens on the market that truly works and helps protect you from check and document fraud.

Finally, if you decide to order checks through your bank DO NOT have them mailed to your home; instead, have the checks delivered to your bank for you to pick up.

CHAPTER EIGHT
Identity Theft

Theft of a person's identity occurs when personal information, such as your social security number or driver's license number, is obtained and used to gain credit, merchandise or specific services. This breach of security could be made by someone you know, like a family member, or a total stranger. It makes no difference who the perpetrator is; the act is a crime.

In February 2012, *Consumer Reports Money Adviser* published an article online titled: *"Debunking the Hype Over ID Theft - You Don't Need a Costly Service to Protect Your Good Name."*[45] In this article it revealed that, in 2010 alone, fifty million people subscribed to some type of identity theft protection. These services generally cost between $100 and $300 a year and generate a whopping $4.5 billion a year in revenue.

While no doubt identity theft is a serious problem, the *Consumer Reports* article also stated: "More than eighty percent of what's been called identity theft involves fraudulent charges on existing accounts, according to the U.S. Department of Justice, but in most cases a cardholder's liability is limited to $50 for a lost or stolen credit card. For debit cards, liability for an unauthorized transaction is limited to $50 if it's reported within two business days of the date a cardholder learns of it. After two days, liability can climb to $500 or more, but many banks provide additional voluntary protections."

What may be shocking to you is that, according to the Federal Trade Commission (FTC), in 2000, 19 percent of all victims of identity theft had a personal relationship with the thief and 10 percent of those thieves were family members!

What's relatively rare is "new account" and "personal information" ID theft, in which someone uses your name, birthdate, and Social Security number to open new credit accounts, tap your health insurance, earn taxable income, or commit crimes in your name. Only 765,000 households were victims of this form of ID theft in 2010, according to the Bureau of Justice, which means the chance of it happening to you is less than one percent a year.

Go online and review the information found at http://www.stopfraud.gov. This website will inform you of all the various types of fraud that are occurring and give you resources on how to avoid becoming a victim. In order to prevent identity theft from happening to you, it would also be wise for you to begin the practice of periodically checking your credit report with all three credit bureaus. You can do this by going online to the website Annual Credit Report at www.annualcreditreport.com.

"AnnualCreditReport.com is a centralized service for consumers to request free annual credit reports. It was created by the three nationwide consumer credit reporting companies - Equifax, Experian and TransUnion. AnnualCreditReport.com provides consumers with the secure means to request and obtain a free credit report once every 12 months from each of the three nationwide consumer credit reporting companies in accordance with the Fair and Accurate Credit Transactions Act (FACT Act)."

"AnnualCreditReport.com offers consumers a fast and convenient way to request, view and print their credit reports in a secure Internet environment. They also provide options to request reports by telephone and by mail. AnnualCreditReport.com is the only service authorized by Equifax, Experian and TransUnion for this purpose. The three nationwide consumer credit reporting companies have always encouraged consumers to regularly review their credit reports."[46]

To receive your free annual credit report from Innovis you can go online to their website at https://www.innovis.com/InnovisWeb/index.html

The Unthinkable Happens

If you have been a victim of identity theft, there are some immediate actions that you need to take to help stop any additional damage from occurring. First, call all the credit agencies and file an initial fraud alert, which is free. Technically if you call one agency they are supposed to notify the others, but it would be to your benefit if you have documentation that you contacted all of them yourself.

You need to be aware that an initial fraud alert stays in effect for a total of ninety days. You have to renew it after ninety days if you want to continue having this higher alert status on your account. To prevent ANY activity, you may opt for a full credit freeze, but this may be too extreme, depending on your circumstances. You should discuss your options with each agency.

Second, order a copy of your credit report to see if there are new accounts that have been opened or if you see any unusual activity. Next, create an identity theft report. You should also create a very detailed paper trail to document all that you have done and are doing. Make sure you have a written logbook in which you record the date, time and telephone number of everyone you talked with concerning your credit theft.

Anytime you send anything by mail, make sure whoever receives the document has to sign for it and that you have a record of it being delivered. Make sure you send only certified copies of documents and not the originals. Also make sure you keep track of any specific deadlines that you need to respond by. Finally, you need to create an identity theft report: "An identity theft report gives you some important rights that can help you recover from the theft. To create one, file a complaint with the FTC and print your identity theft affidavit. Use that to file a police report and create your identity theft report."[47]

To learn more, you can download Taking Charge: What to Do If Your Identity Is Stolen: "The FTC's updated and comprehensive guide for victims of identity theft, including to-do lists, contact information, blank forms and sample letters." http://www.consumer.ftc.gov/articles/pdf-0009-taking-charge.pdf

Review Your Credit Card Statement

Check your credit card statements and debit card statements throughout the month to monitor activity. Most credit card companies now offer the option to receive texts or e-mails to notify you of possible fraudulent charges so problems can be addressed immediately. This extra service is free.

Too often we get in a hurry and do not take the time to review all the charges on our credit card statement and just blindly pay the bill! This is not only unwise but can be costly. Many times people who are trying to commit fraud will charge a small amount on your card to see if the charge is accepted before putting in a charge for a bigger amount.

Protecting Your Wealth ~ Investments

When it comes to the topic of managing your money and building wealth there are plenty of so called "financial porn experts" that will give you advice. Many will lead you to believe that if you follow just a few simple steps you will be on the road to making money in no time so you can retire. Life is not that simple; it never has been, nor should you believe it to be. As individuals we are not always logical in our thinking. Likewise, how we invest and how investments react do not always match up to something you might think is logical. There is not one set formula that works one hundred percent of the time.

How we act, or react for that matter, can be driven by fear or greed. Investing means riding the waves, which for many of us makes us more than just a little seasick. To be perfectly honest, most of us have never been taught to handle this psychological nightmare. If the stock market crashes and we see our assets drop in half, many want to pull everything out of fear of losing it all.

By searching on the Internet, there appears to be no definitive data that will state the percentage of people who invest in the stock market and lose money doing so. I can only theorize that the reason no such data is readily available is that the financial industry does not want you to know the answer. However, life itself is not risk-free, so why should we think our investments should be? The older I get, the more pessimistic I become on believing what I hear or read from darn near everyone.

I can't understand how, as a country, we can owe what we do, borrow what we borrow, and spend the amount we spend and still be positive about the future. The U.S. Debt Clock: http://www.usdebtclock.org/ tells the story. At some point the craziness will have to end. What will ultimately cause this is hard to imagine, but it is illogical to think we can continue on this path and not expect an ultimate crash at some point.

So, where does this leave the average person? What should you do? First and foremost, live your life within or beneath your means. Choosing to do this is not going to be easy. Unlike the government, you will not be able to run your life owing more money than you make for very long if that is the path you choose.

Unfortunately, most people have a misconception that any rise in the stock market must somehow be directly tied to the economy. Yet the world famous oracle of Omaha Warren Buffet probably said it best when he was quoted as saying, "If you knew what was going to happen in the economy, you still wouldn't necessarily know what was going to happen in the stock market."

The reason any investor puts money in the stock market, whereby taking a risk, is for an expectation of a potential return. We all would love to believe that everything is logical. But investing in the stock market and the way stocks react is far from logical. Tell me, is the glass half empty or half full? Perception, for most, becomes reality.

The following is a list of questions you need to ask yourself before investing your hard earned money.

What is happening today that makes you feel confident about the future? Are the general living conditions for the average American going up or down? Are things in general better or worse? What is the ability for new college graduates to find a job paying a decent wage? Has your standard of living gone up or down and kept pace with inflation? Are you able to save money for retirement, or has the word itself become obsolete or at the very least taken on a new meaning? Are we in an economic recovery period? Hindsight is unforgiving, and it will tell us in due time.

Recently, the mainstream media reported that a whopping 57 percent of Americans had less than $25,000 in savings and investments. Yet only 28 percent thought they would not have enough money to retire comfortably.

I guess some folks think the Tooth Fairy is going to come through after all! Break out the marshmallows, folks, and huddle around the fire. This "bedtime story" that is about to unfold for many Americans should undoubtedly make some have nightmares. If not, then they are already asleep!

Social Security

No one is going to make sure that the information provided to the government is accurate except you. It is imperative that you protect yourself by checking online with the Social Security Administration at http://www.socialsecurity.gov/ and review the information they have recorded on an annual basis.

This document will show your annual earnings history and give you an estimated monthly payment for full retirement or early retirement based on your age. The statement also gives details of benefits if you become disabled or survivor benefits in case of your death.

Paper or Plastic – Cash or Credit

Most people today use a credit or debit card versus making most of their purchases with cash. In fact, we are quickly becoming a cashless society. Debit cards, in many cases, have replaced handwritten checks.

In 2012, the Rasmussen Reports™ conducted a survey that found 43 percent of people went an entire week without spending cash. Yet reports dating back to 1979 show that, by using plastic, consumers are likely to spend more than if they had to shell out cash for their purchases. In essence, it becomes more real seeing the cash leave your hands versus just swiping a card. Another wrinkle in this equation is the fact that one in twelve low-income Americans do not have a checking or savings account, so they do not have access to a debit card unless they opt for the prepaid version, which can be costly due to the fees associated with purchasing the card.[48]

If you are one of those who only use a credit or debit card, ask yourself what would happen if there were a catastrophic electronic failure? What would you do if you could ONLY make a transaction by paying with cash? The sad reality is that most people would be royally screwed, because they have no backup plan of extra cash tucked away for emergencies.

Lost Money

Unfortunately, there is not just ONE website or place you can go to find all the unclaimed monies that could be owed to you or one of your relatives. However, below are several common places where money that is owed to you may likely be hiding. You need to make sure to search these sources regardless of whether you think money might be owed to you. You might end up with a nice surprise!

Escheat and Unclaimed Property

Each state maintains a list of unclaimed funds and properties and the information for your specific state and how to search this list can be found on the following website: http://www.unclaimed.org/.

Pensions

Unclaimed pensions of former employees from businesses that have gone out of business can be searched at this website: http://search.pbgc.gov/mp/.

Tax Refunds

Tax refunds generally fall into two categories: those that are unclaimed refunds and those that are undeliverable refunds. If you think you have either you should call the IRS toll-free assistance line at 800-829-1040.

Mortgages

Most people incur a mortgage when purchasing their home. If you happen to have a FHA-insured mortgage then you likely paid for "mortgage insurance" to cover you in the event that you could not make the payment. If you are like a lot of people, you were successful in making the payment and are eligible for a refund from the Department of Housing and Urban Development (HUD). The catch to all this is that you have to apply to receive the refund; it does not automatically revert back to you! To see if you are eligible go to this website now: http://www.hud.gov/offices/hsg/comp/refunds/index.cfm

Savings Bonds

Literally billions of dollars each year are lost because people have savings bonds that were purchased years ago that they have forgotten and that are no longer earning interest. U.S. Department of the Treasury, Bureau of the Public Debt has a website they maintain that you should search. Go to http://www.treasuryhunt.gov/.

CHAPTER NINE
Home Security

Found Your Dream Home?

It is an exciting time when you finally are able to find a place you can call your own.

However, the excitement can turn into a tragic nightmare if you don't first protect yourself. Before leaping into a home purchase, you need to not just rely on a real estate agent telling you this is the perfect place for you. You need to look at your new possible "dream home" through the eyes of an investigator. Check the location at all times of the day and night. Does the area appear safe, or do you see graffiti or any neighbor's yard that appears to be unkempt? Homes within three blocks of major thoroughfares, those on a cul-de-sac, as well as those adjacent to parks or wooded areas sometimes are deemed to be higher risk than others.

Before buying any home, make sure to visit with your local law enforcement agency and request a copy of the area crime report for your neighborhood. If you have a smart phone go the App store and search "crime map." There you will find various Apps, many for free, that will give you up-to-date information on crime in your area. One App I've found most helpful is RAIDS Online Mobile by Blair Analytics.

Another important step you need to take to protect yourself is looking online at the National Sex Offender Public Registry (NSOPR) at http://www.nsopw.gov. According to the website "NSOPW is the only U.S. government website that links public state, territorial, and tribal sex offender registries from one national search site. Parents, employers, and other concerned residents can utilize the website's search tool to identify location information on sex offenders residing, working, and attending school, not only in their own neighborhoods but in other nearby states and communities. In addition, the website provides visitors with information about sexual abuse and how to protect themselves and loved ones from potential victimization."

When you purchase a home, most people are aware of the need to first have a title search done to make sure that they are getting a property deed that is in fact free and clear. It is also common for people to have a home inspection prior to the purchase to identify any deficiencies that might not be easily seen. Before you hire someone to undertake this process, it would be advisable to look at the guidelines from The International Association of Certified Home Inspectors (InterNACHI), which can be found online at http://www.nachi.org/sop.htm

Next Steps

A home inspection is just the first of many steps you should take to make sure this property is the right choice for you. Beyond a home inspection, you need to concern yourself with identifying any and all possible hazards and the risks they might pose. These include, but are not limited to, natural hazards and environmental hazards. Understand your ability to insure the property and find out any restrictions that might be associated with your location.

The following is a checklist you may want to use in the assessment of your property to help you identify any risk factors that might be present.

Natural Hazards:

___ Coastal and/or Riverine Erosion

___ Dam and Levee Failures

___ Droughts and Heat Waves

___ Earthquakes and Fault Line Locations

___ Floods

___ Hurricanes and Coastal Storms

___ Landslides and Sink Holes

___ Severe Storms and Tornadoes

___ Tsunamis

___ Volcanoes

___ Wildfires

___ Winter Storms and Freezes

Environmental Hazards:

__Asbestos

__Arsenic

__Electrical (High Voltage Lines and/or Substations)

__Formaldehyde

__Lead based paint

__Leaking underground storage

__Methane

__Mold

__Radiation

__Radon gas

You should make an inquiry to identify any Environmental Protection Agency (EPA) contamination sites in the area, as well as all major governmental and/or industrial facilities that have either air or hazard waste permits. This would include identifying the closest water treatment plant that might use chlorine. Identify the closest nuclear facility and any coal-fired electric facility in the area. Is there any hydraulic fracturing or "fracking" taking place in the area? Is there any blasting done in the area?

Additionally, you need to be aware of the distance to the interstate and the closest railway. Inquire as to the general times of use and the types of cargo transported. All locations of any current and/or former military sites, commercial and private airport sites, and potential risk of crash zones should be identified.

In looking at the property itself, you need to be aware of any homeowner covenants, conservation easements, utility easements, existing or abandoned underground storage tanks, or potential wildlife protection zones. The city or town may also have specific ordinances that could restrict how many people are allowed to live in your home or if vehicles are allowed to be parked on the grass or on the street.

An additional inspection will likely be needed to check for any possible infestation of insects or rodents, and you will also want to ensure that the home has no mold, mildew or other fungi growing in, around, on top of or underneath the home.

If the home location is not connected to a municipal water and/or sewer system then you should make sure the ground can support a fully operational septic system and receive the proper permits. Also, regardless of your drinking water source, you should verify your water quality.

The following are a few products that may help you in your home inspection process:

Where Can I Get a Radon Test Kit? | Radon | US Environmental Protection Agency
http://www.epa.gov/radon/radontest.html

PRO-LAB® http://prolabinc.com has a full line of home test kits to test for the following hazards: asbestos, carbon monoxide, lead in paint and dust, mold, radon and water quality.

3M™ offers a product called LeadCheck™ Swabs:
http://leadcheck.com. These swabs will detect
lead on painted wood, metal, vinyl, plastic,
drywall and plaster.

Purtest® www.purtest.com has a wide range of
water testing kits that can identify the following:
alkalinity, arsenic, bacteria, chlorine, iron, lead,
nitrate, nitrite, pH, pesticides and water hardness.

Industrial Test Systems, Inc. (ITS) http://www.
sensafe.com offers a wide variety of water quality
test kits.

Insurance

When it comes to your possessions, a serious discussion should take place concerning the topic of insurance.
It is amazing that you can insure practically anything!

Homeowner's insurance, personal property insurance, life insurance, cars, boats, ATVs, you name it
and it probably can be insured for loss or theft. Most
people are covered with personal liability insurance, but
did you know you can also have excess liability insurance to cover you for $1 million or more for those
worst-case scenarios?

So what is your biggest threat? Do you really know
factually if what you have chosen to cover by buying
insurance is actually covered in full? Be honest with
yourself! Most folks cringe when you say this because
deep down inside we likely have opted at some point to
not read all the fine details in the contracts and relied

on an agent to tell us what we need and assume it is covered. Through the process we have mainly worried about how much it costs.

As boring as it might seem to you now, it is best to know if you are covered in case the sewer line backs up or your toilet overflows when you are out of town. Otherwise, you might find out that you were not covered for that disaster after all. Most homeowners' policies have coverage limits on what they pay for items like collectibles, guns and silverware. To be covered for those you might need a rider added to your policy.

Note that sinkholes or events like floods and earthquakes are not typically covered as part of your regular homeowner's insurance policy. All this and more needs to be discussed at length with your insurance agent. The time to ask is before, not after, you need help.

Have a CLUE® to What You are Getting Into!

In accordance with the Fair Credit Reporting Act, the owner of the property, as well as the insurer or lender, can obtain a Comprehensive Loss Underwriting Exchange Report or C.L.U.E.® for short. This report discloses the five-year history of the insurance losses the property in question may have incurred. If no losses were associated with this property it will state that no losses occurred.

Before you consider making an offer to buy your dream home you might first make sure you will be able to insure the property, as well as know in advance if the property you are purchasing had sustained any damages in the past. It would be helpful to know if a broken water pipe upstairs previously flooded the lower portion of the house and may have caused mold problems.

Any offer to purchase should be contingent on receiving a positive C.L.U.E.® report before closing. You can order a C.L.U.E.® Home Seller's Disclosure Report by going to the LexisNexis® website at https://personal reports.lexisnexis.com/homesellers_disclosure_report/ landing.jsp

Ignorance is Bliss

We often ignore security concerns until after a break-in occurs in the neighborhood. Most burglaries happen between 10 a.m. and 3 p.m. when most people are away from home and are at work; however, break-ins can happen at any time!

A true story that recently occurred in my city involved a late night break-in of an occupied home in a residential neighborhood. The husband and wife were awakened at night when they heard a noise coming from the garage. When the man went to investigate, he was shot and killed. Later, the thieves were apprehended and prosecuted for murder. They said they thought the house was abandoned when they tried to break in.

Action Steps

Making your home look "lived in" is an important part of home safety and security. There are many ways to achieve this through lighting, by using motion sensors, and timers that turn lights on and off at set or random intervals. Also, it is important to keep your blinds or drapes as you normally would, but still restrict the ability for someone to come up to the window and peer in to see what is inside.

At night one of the best lights you can have on a timer is the one in the bathroom. People obviously have to use the bathroom at all times of the day and night, and this light can leave some doubt in a criminal's mind if someone might be home.

Place in your yard a sign stating you have a home security system, regardless if this is a fact or not. Make sure the sign identifies a company that is local and recognized. Perception can become a reality to a criminal, and the goal for this is for them to move on to choose another target that looks more inviting. However, do not completely rely on "fake" security! Crooks might be dumb, but most are not totally stupid. Remember that fake blinking cameras or a window sticker will only be so effective and do nothing in the case of a real emergency.

If you leave for an extended period of time, make sure your mail and newspapers are retrieved. Having a house sitter is a good idea to make sure your home looks lived in, as well as keeping your shades or curtains as you normally would instead of having everything look sealed. Finally, if possible, have a neighbor park a car in your driveway so a casual passerby would not know if anyone was home or away.

Keep your grass cut and make sure it is done if needed when you are away. If it is the time of year when there is snow falling, have your driveway and walkway shoveled. Trim back tall bushes that create natural hiding spots, especially around trashcans. Make sure to cut low branches of trees so they cannot be easily climbed to access second-story balconies or windows. Look carefully at any trellis or gutter work and identify if they pose any type of security risk. Shrubbery should not block the view out any window and should be no taller than three feet high. Planting something that is thorny or a plant with briers makes for a good natural defense from people trying to hide. Do what it takes to make entry into your home more difficult.

A dead giveaway that no one is home is the morning paper sitting in the driveway all afternoon or an over-stuffed mailbox. Instead of stopping deliveries, ask a trusted neighbor to pick up any newspapers, mail and packages in your absence.

Burglars are known to look for notes left on the door to notify you of a potential package delivery or actual packages sitting on the porch. Not only can a package be stolen, but once someone has your name they can look that name up in the local phone book to see if it is listed. Burglars have been known to call the phone number to make sure you are not at home before breaking into your house. For this reason you may wish to have an unlisted phone number. You could also forward your calls so that someone answers the phone if it rings. If this is not practical then, at the very least, turn any phone or answering machine ringer as low as possible so that it would be difficult to detect from outside.

It is important to remember that most burglars are opportunists, and if entry is gained via a glass window or door then it will be achieved by tossing a heavy object into them. With this in mind, it is best to keep your yard free of any heavy rocks or loose bricks. Finally, as a friendly reminder, remember if you have any repair work done in your home make sure you always check to ensure no windows or doors were left unlocked. If you do find this is the case, be cautious.

A Hidden Advantage

If entry is gained into your home, you need to have a plan in place to protect yourself first and your property second. As far as your property is concerned, the first step in this process is to have a photographic and a written record of all your valuables, including the model, serial number, date of purchase and the original receipt.

The best possible chance to recover any stolen property occurs when the item is marked so that it can be later identified. The most common ways to mark an item are an engraving pen to etch into the item itself or, the less destructive and more covert method, an ultraviolet marking pen. The writing with the ultraviolet pen is invisible and is only revealed by using a black light. Another product available is called COP DOTS found at www.copdots.com, a pen like device that dispenses micro dots that you can use to mark up to 50 items with an identifiable unique ID that is supported by law enforcement.

Mark all the big-ticket items that are often stolen: laptops, game consoles, televisions, and stereo equipment, as well as items like grills and lawnmowers. If using an ultraviolet pen or engraver consider marking items using your last name and driver's license number. Never use your social security number when marking an item of value.

Again make sure all the recorded information about your valuables and photos are placed in a secure location, not on a personal computer that is likely to be stolen. If you have expensive electronic items, the user manuals often provide additional information you need for insurance companies when you are establishing a loss.

While it might sound a bit extreme, consider having "burglar traps" that you place in your home or in an outside storage shed that create a noise. Probably one of the cheapest ways to accomplish this is to use a standalone, battery-operated motion detector that uses an infrared beam, sometimes called an "electronic eye," that when broken sounds either an alarm or tone.

Be aware that you do NOT want to have any trap device that is life threatening, because you would be held liable, even if the person was trying to break into your property. Another option is to consider purchasing a cheap safe that you place in your master bedroom on the floor unbolted and in plain sight as a decoy. NOTE: The master bedroom is one of the first places a burglar goes when they break into your home looking for valuables to steal.

Make sure your dummy safe contains a few heavy bricks and a few hundred loose pennies so it makes noise when moved. In addition, have a fake jewelry box with an added twist. Your fake jewelry items are sprinkled with a theft detection powder!

This powder can be purchased for around $20 and is designed to be dusted on items you expect the suspect will handle. Search online using the term "Visible Theft Detection Stain Powder" to find the lowest cost provider. This powder works by acting with the amino acids in the body and leaves the person's hands with a bright purple stain that is very difficult to wash off and typically lasts for several days.

If you are using this powder on items you place outside exposed to the elements, you may want to mix the powder into a paste with Vaseline so it will hold up better in these conditions. Note that using this powder may also discolor the items you are placing it on.

A more covert powder is an UV ultraviolet powder that will stain the hands of anyone who touches the treated items but remains invisible. The hands will glow when a UV light is applied. One place you can look to see all the options that are available is LDP LLC - http://www.maxmax.com/aSpecialtyInks.htm

One more tip: If you have a child's room in your home, this is one of the last places most burglars look. Think about having a concealed place in this room to store valuables.

A Safe Room

If you follow all the recommendations outlined in this book, practically every room in your home will be safer than it was before. However, the concept of a safe room refers to a place where you and your family can go in the event of an emergency. Some people have these for weather emergencies, like a hurricane or tornado, and others in the event of a home invasion. If your room is intended for weather protection then you need to consult with a structural engineer to understand what type of weather impact your home can withstand and what structural changes need to be made. If a new home is being built, people will often have a concrete room structure created – similar to a bank vault.

More common is the idea of having a room that is fortified so that, in the event of a home invasion, when escape is not possible, everyone can gather in this area for safety. Many times a safe room is close to or part of the master bedroom. Regardless, any and all doors need to be either solid wood or metal, and the doorframes need to be solid as well. The locks need to go well beyond the common door latch, and you need to make sure that you have a deadbolt installed, preferably with a solid metal box plate and long screws that anchor into the doorjamb. If your safe room is upstairs and you have windows, then you also need to have an emergency solid metal chain ladder that is rated to withstand 1,000 pounds so that it can support more than one person on the ladder at the time.

If you have an alarm system, your safe room needs to have a control panel to the alarm in the room as well as a secondary means of signaling for help. This might include a key fob that could activate a car panic alarm, an air can operated air horn, a bullhorn or some other noisemaking device. This room needs to have a phone, but you should not rely only on a hard-wired line but have a cell phone as well. Even a cell phone that has been deactivated is capable of dialing 911 in the event of an emergency if the phone is charged. Make sure you keep a spare set of keys to your home in your safe room you could toss out a window to the police in the event they need to unlock a door. You also need to have a fire extinguisher, as well as any other personal protection devices you feel comfortable having.

Anti-Climb Paint

While I have yet to find this in the United States, it can be found in the U.K. and really, when you think about it, this is a brilliant idea!

"Anti-climb paint is also known as anti-vandal, anti-burglar, anti-intruder or anti-scale paint. It is basically a thick glutinous paint with a similar appearance to smooth gloss paint, however, when applied it does not dry and remains slippery indefinitely, preventing an intruder from gaining a foothold. Not only does it not dry, it is also extremely difficult to remove from clothing so acting as an excellent deterrent to possible intruders. This makes anti-climb paint a very simple, economic and effective way of protecting your property from intruders."[49]

Operation Identification – Proactive Deterrent

This program, which has helped homeowners prevent crime for more than 30 years, is effective because it allows police officers to detect, identify and return lost or stolen items to their owner. According to the website, "The Operation ID program involves marking or engraving property with an identifying number and displaying a window decal to discourage burglary and theft. The ideal identifying number is your state issued Driver's License number which is easily recognized and traced by law enforcement."

Following are the three important steps required to participate in the Operation ID program:

1. Mark property or valuables with an identifying mark, preferably your driver's license state abbreviation followed by the number: Example: CA-B1234567
2. Inventory your marked property on a form with descriptions including brand, model number, and serial number. Keep it in a safe place.
3. Display the Operation ID decal on windows ONLY AFTER items 1 and 2 have been completed to show your participation in the program and to discourage burglary.[50]

You may want to contact your local law enforcement agency to learn more about Operation ID and what they can offer you for free. You can also learn more online by visiting the National Neighborhood Watch Institute (NNWI) website at http://www.nnwi.org.

Make sure to look at the additional materials they offer that can not only help you be better prepared against theft but also against other disasters. Specifically I would recommend you taking a look at the handbook titled: DASH – Disaster And Survivor Handbook.

Happy and Sad Occasions

Many people, even the ultra-private, tend to make announcements to the world on various occasions. A few of those include weddings, funerals, and the sale of homes. Unfortunately, this has the potential to be noticed by some people you would rather not know – namely burglars.

If you read in a church bulletin that a specific member of the church is in the hospital or read in the local newspaper that someone has died or is engaged to be married, this information unfortunately can be used to target the home for a break-in.

Obituary announcements include the time and place of a visitation as well as the time of the funeral and/or burial services. It is imperative that someone trusted stay behind at these times so the home of the deceased is not left unattended.

Offering a home for sale when the owner's possessions are still inside poses a unique threat. An open house showing can also pose a threat. It's possible for two would-be thieves to attend the show while one distracts the realtor and the other walks into several rooms to purposefully leave doors and windows unlocked.

Answering Machine Safety

We might not think that a device that is supposed to help us might actually pose a risk to our safety, but it can. When you record a message DO NOT say, "I'm sorry I'm not in right now." You are just telling the burglar your home is empty. Instead, simply say: "Thank you for calling, please leave us a message," regardless if you are single or not. It is even more important if you are woman living alone that you refer to the plural versus the singular.

As mentioned before, you need to make sure that both your answering machine and telephone ringers throughout your house are at the lowest level possible. You want to make it difficult, if not impossible, to hear from outside. The reason is you do not want someone who is thinking about breaking in standing at your outside doorway hearing the phone ring and verifying that you are indeed not home.

Mailbox Safety

First and foremost, your name should never be displayed on your mailbox. Also, you should refrain from having a name plaque at the front of your home. You should consider having your street address number marked on your mailbox and on the curb in front of your home, if this is applicable to your situation. It is recommended that you paint a white 6" X 8"rectangle and use black paint to stencil your house number in block letters. Check with your local city or county agency to make sure this meets any requirements they may have.

Just as your trash can be a wealth of information, so can your mailbox. If a person knows your name they can look it up in the phone book. If you are listed then they have your phone number, which they can call to see if you are home in an effort to time when they might break in.

On a positive note, many people have switched to paying bills online or having the amount owed automatically drafted from an account. Despite this precaution, you might still receive various statements containing personal information that can be easily intercepted.

Most of us don't have a locking mailbox system; there is one inexpensive product that has been invented that you can use to retrofit your existing mailbox called the GrayDoor® Residential Mailbox Insert Locking System at http://www.mailboxsafety.com/. Installing this insert, according to the inventor, is "like having a PO box at your curbside."

If you decide to upgrade your mailbox completely, you may want to consider the mailboxes offered by the Steel Mailbox Co. at http://www.steelmailbox.com/. Instead of a key, their locking mailboxes are digital and more like a mini safe, but they still allow letters to be inserted by the mail carrier.

Let There Be Light

Regardless of whether you have street lighting, you should still consider installing motion floodlights, dusk-to-dawn lighting, and/or low voltage LED lights at your home.

A key to any lighting project is determining where the shadows are at night and lighting up those areas. Be sure that any lighting you install does not have an adverse effect with neighbors close by. Nothing can be more frustrating for a neighbor than to have a spotlight shining into his or her bedroom at night.

Heath/Zenith at http://www.heath-zenith.com makes an entire line of dusk-to-dawn motion-activated lighting. Their lantern style is one that you might typically use at your front door. This light detects motion and light in a 360-degree pattern. Their patented technology called DualBrite® allows the light to come on at dusk and operate at half power for three or six hours or until dawn. If full light is needed, you can manually override this feature. If motion is detected the light activates to the brightest setting for one, five or ten minutes, depending on the setting you choose. After that time period the light drops back to half power and remains lit according to your settings of either three or six hours or until dawn. Motion sensor lighting should not just be used at your front door, but also your driveway and any back door locations.

Consider having lights on timers in various parts of your home to turn on and off lights at specific times or, better yet, random times. The overall goal is to make your home look "lived in" regardless of whether you are home at the time or not. To achieve this goal you can install plug-in timers that you can plug a lamp into or you can opt to install a device like a seven-day digital timer by Utilitech that can be found at most home improvement stores. This wall timer can be set to turn your overhead lights on and off up to seven times per day.

You might consider turning on a radio or television or use a product like Fake TV, http://www.faketv.com. This has a dawn-to-dusk feature that uses light patterns to simulate a television being turned on for four hours, seven hours or until dawn.

The brighter and more lived-in your home looks, and the more visible your house is at night, the better and more of a deterrent it is.

**Note: When possible make sure flood lights as well as other lighting is out of normal reach so the bulbs cannot easily be unscrewed.

Fencing

On one hand, a privacy fence might make you feel secure from the prying eyes of neighbors, but it can also work in reverse and help conceal someone trying to break into your home. The best way to protect yourself from a simple threat is to make sure you secure all entry points with a lock to make access to your fenced yard more difficult. A chain link fence is not only a good physical barrier, but a psychological one as well. Anyone thinking about attempting a burglary will be thinking about how easy or hard it will be to escape undetected with larger bulky electronics. You may also want to put video cameras or a separate motion sensor at the gate entryway into the fence that notifies someone in the home with an alert tone. Another deterrent that makes a person think before entering is a simple

"Beware of Dog" sign, regardless of whether you actually have a dog or not.

The more extreme option might be an electric fence or maybe even a fence that incorporates barbwire. However, before installing either type of fencing, you need to consult with your insurance agent to identify any liability concerns. Also, make sure to check with your municipal or other governmental agencies to see if they have additional requirements you must meet when installing such a fence, such as posting signage notifying those who attempt entry of the risk of injury. Sad, but true.

Driveway Safety

If you are located in a secluded area that has a long driveway to your residence, you might want to consider having a driveway alarm system to notify you if someone is approaching your home. There is a wide array of both wired and wireless technology available depending on your situation.

Always remember when you approach your unlocked car that anyone could be inside! Be wary of leaving devices like a GPS in plain view on the dash of your car or attached to your window. Checkbooks are an easy target and should never be left in your car. All this screams to the criminal, "Take me!" It can't be stressed enough that you need to lock your car doors at all times when you are in your car or leave the car unattended, regardless of the amount of time you might be away. This is also true at the gas pump. You should also think about installing a locking fuel cap on all your vehicles, whether the fuel door compartment on your vehicle locks or not. Having the cap sealed and locked will slow someone down who is trying to siphon fuel out, or worse, pour something in your tank to render your vehicle inoperable.

There are a number of security devices that you can use to make your car less likely to be stolen. Some of those devices include a wheel locking system – a device that attaches to your brake pedal – as well as a circular band that fits around your steering column and wheel-locking devices. Furthermore, there are additional locks for sliding glass windows, spare tires and batteries. Some choose a more covert approach which, instead of preventing a vehicle from being taken, can help locate a vehicle by using a remote tracking device. A well-known device that boasts a 90 percent recovery rate is the LoJack™, which not only locates a car that is stolen but can provide an early warning notification via e-mail or text message if the vehicle is stolen without a pass key present. To learn more go to the following website: http://www.lojack.com/Home.

Once in your car, the doors should be locked at all times, especially at a stoplight, and also in a parking lot even if you only plan to be away from your car a few minutes. It should go without saying, but texting and driving is a big no-no and illegal in some states. Even talking on the phone hands-free can cause a problem; we all can get so easily distracted. Finally, if you are one of those who won't wear a seatbelt the question I have to ask you is, "Why?" Your life is more important than a wrinkled outfit, don't you think?

You also need to carefully consider all the items you have in your car. Are they really necessary? Do they encourage someone to try to break into your car? What security risk do they pose if they were in the hands of a criminal? The reason for these questions is that gaining access to the inside of your car is not very difficult. The fact of the matter is that 98 percent of all car doors can be opened by a simple tool that you can buy off the Internet for less than $60 called the "BigEasy." This device slides through the top of your window and presses open your automatic door lock. Another lockout tool that has been around for a while is more commonly known as a "Slim Jim." This thin strip of metal is inserted between the car's window and door to pull up the rods that operate the door lock to gain entry. There are other tools of the trade that locksmiths use that the average person can buy off the Internet without much problem.

Garage Security

Your garage door is another large access point that people often ignore. Make sure when you move in, even if the home is brand new, that you change the code that opens your garage door.

From a security perspective, a solid garage door is better than one that has windows or panels that allow someone to see inside. If your garage door does have windows, keep them covered. If your garage is attached to your house, make sure the external garage door is as sturdy and fortified as the door on the front of your home.

Also, be aware that leaving your garage door open for long periods of time extends an invitation to unwanted guests, especially those that drive by in your neighborhood looking for easy targets. The more expensive toys you have on display outside, the more the criminal could believe that inside your home would be even more expensive items as well. As best you can, keep things like your bicycles, that big tool chest, riding lawn mower and gas grill out of sight.

Another point of safety that should be mentioned is not storing gas cans in your garage, or having lots of oily rags or piles of old newspapers stacked about. All these are fire hazards that should be avoided.

Once closed, your garage door needs to be secure and not easily pried open from the outside. Most motorized garage doors come with one or more battery-operated remote control openers. The threat comes when you leave your remote control unattended in your unlocked car in the driveway. The solution may frustrate some, but you should consider removing the garage door remote control from your car and, in its place, buy a keychain remote that you take with you every time you leave and lock your car.

When you go on vacation, if you can, turn off the power to your garage door altogether. If the door motor plugs into a socket in the ceiling, an easy solution, beyond throwing a breaker switch, would be to buy a handheld transmitter and plug in the receiver that you might typically use to turn off holiday lights. One click of the switch and the power to your garage door is disabled. Many garage doors have additional side latches that can slide into place to help lock the door in the closed position. Another way to make the door secure is to place a padlock shackle through a hole where the door rollers travel, locking the door into place.

Another security product to consider is a product called the PJD Garage Defender. This device is an angled bar that is wedged against the center portion of your garage door and secured in place with a bracket that is mounted on the concrete floor of your garage that can be locked as well.

Open Sesame

The automatic garage door first began in the 1920s. Many were opened using a keypad attached to a post. Later wireless remote switches were used; however, these early transmitters and receivers only operated on a few frequencies so security quickly became an issue, with a good possibility that your neighbor could open your garage door as well as his own. To address this problem, a system was developed where the owner could manually program a security code using six to twelve switches in different positions that would be programmed on the transmitter and the receiver. Later a device was invented called a "code grabber," making it possible for the criminal element to record the transmitted frequency when the door was opened. Again, to thwart this security breach, a rolling code method was developed that transmitted on a wider range of frequencies and changed the code used each time the door was opened.[51]

In addition to security concerns, the need for entrapment protection has been addressed by the U.S. Consumer Product Safety Commission:

"In an effort to reduce the number of deaths to children who become entrapped under garage doors with automatic openers, the U.S. Consumer Product Safety Commission (CPSC) issued final rules for automatic residential garage door openers. The rules, which will be published in the Federal Register, include revised entrapment protection requirements for all automatic residential garage door openers manufactured on or after January 1, 1993 for sale in the United States. The rules also include certification requirements and recordkeeping requirements for garage door opener manufacturers.

"The entrapment protection requirements are part of a Congressional mandate in the Consumer Product Safety Improvement Act of 1990. The legislation requires that automatic residential garage door openers manufactured on or after January 1, 1991 conform to the entrapment protection requirements of the Underwriters Laboratories (UL) Standard for Safety, UL 325.

"The legislation also requires that residential garage door openers manufactured on or after January 1, 1993 comply with additional entrapment protection requirements developed by UL. The rules issued specify these additional entrapment protection requirements. The revised standard requires that residential garage door openers contain one of the following:

"External entrapment protection device, such as an 'electric eye' which 'sees' an object obstructing the door without having actual contact with the object. Another similar device would be a door edge sensor. The door edge sensor acts much like the door edge sensors on elevator doors.

"Constant contact control button which is a wall-mounted button requiring a person to hold in the control button continuously for the door to close completely. If the button is released before the door closes, the door would reverse and open to the highest position. The remote control transmitter will not close the door with this option.

"Additionally, all newly-manufactured garage door openers must include a sticker warning consumers of the potential entrapment hazard. The sticker is to be placed near the wall mounted control button.

"The entrapment protection requirements are aimed at reducing the potential for entrapment between the edge of the garage door and the floor. Since 1982, the Commission received reports of 54 children between the ages of two and 14 who died after becoming entrapped under doors with automatic garage door openers.

"CPSC urges consumers with automatic garage door openers to test the openers according to the manufacturer's recommendations, to make sure they have a reversing feature. The reversing feature should then be tested monthly. If the door fails to reverse, adjust the door according to the owner's manual or have it inspected by a professional repairman.

"Additionally, owners of automatic garage door openers should teach their children about garage door safety and keep transmitters and remote controls out of children's reach."[52]

Today another threat has surfaced, with a YouTube video that has over a million views showing how easy it is to open a garage door from the outside using a bent coat hanger in less than ten seconds! The method used involves placing a wedge in the top of your garage door and inserting a bent coat hanger, which pulls the emergency release lever to release the door.

There are two ways to prevent this attack. The first is very simple and cheap and involves using an inexpensive plastic zip tie and wrapping it around the lever to hold it firm. Since a simple bent coat hanger does not have the leverage or strength to break the wire, the attack is prevented. In the event of an emergency, you still should be able to jerk down hard enough to break the zip tie if needed to release the door.

The second solution comes by placing a metal cover over the release handle and threading the existing rope release away from release. The product is called SecureShield. "This patent pending design mounts around the emergency release lever and protects it from outside access. It is easy to install and works with most garage doors. Intruders will no longer have the ability to enter your home, giving you peace-of-mind while keeping your family at home safe."[53]

Basement Doors and Windows

Basement doors that lead to a cellar or heating and air handling equipment, as well as windows at ground level, need to be kept secure. Pay close attention and make sure all your outside doors can withstand repeated kicks or attempts to gain entry. Deadbolts are a must! If your basement has a set of steps that lead into your home, then the door going into your basement from your house needs to be an exterior grade door.

Crawl Space Doors

Any door that leads under your house or porch should have the access panel or door secured with a lock. Also, if you have an alarm system, make it a priority to either have those doors hardwired to your system or use a wireless door contact switch.

Fireplace Ash Doors

If you have a fireplace, you need to make sure any cleanout ash door located on the exterior part of your chimney is no larger than sixteen inches wide and eight inches high. Another caution to consider is where you stack your firewood. You should NOT place firewood next to your house near a doorway. Doing so could allow someone to hide behind or use the stack as a stepladder to access a window. Instead, consider placing firewood a safe distance away from your home and visible from all sides.

Storage Sheds

Generally speaking, people store lawn equipment and tools, including ladders, in storage sheds located on the property. These sheds can vary greatly in size and shape, but most of the time they are not constructed with security in mind. Materials used for doors are either thin metal or lightweight wood, often with the hinges exposed. The door handle may lock or there may even be a hasp that allows you to add an extra padlock. Breaking into these buildings is not very difficult.

What might be worse is the fact that some of the items you might actually be storing could be used against you as tools to help with breaking into your home. While you may not be able to avoid this fact, you need to still be aware of it.

There are several things you can do to help protect your belongings. Use floodlights or motion sensor lighting at night so that anyone approaching or standing at the door would be visible. Use a shrouded padlock to make it difficult to cut the lock and cover any windows and secure them shut. Next, with a security pen, mark and inventory what you have in your storage shed and make sure your homeowners' insurance covers any possible losses from unattached buildings on your property. If you have an alarm system, you may want to add a door contact sensor that would alert you if someone tries to force open the door. At the very least you can pick up an inexpensive battery operated door alarm at the dollar store to make noise to potentially scare someone away if the door is opened.

You can always put a security warning sticker or an Operation ID sticker on the door of the shed to make the potential thief think twice before breaking in.

CHAPTER TEN

Safety Around the House

Outdoor Grilling

If you are like a lot of folks you might enjoy grilling outdoors. At this point I'm going to put in a shameless plug for probably one of the most expensive and finest outdoor stainless steel gas grills ever made – The Wilmington Grill: http://www.wilmingtongrill.com.

These ALL stainless steel gas grills are unbelievable, but they are not cheap! The reason I included this recommendation in this book is to say that, while it is important to be secure with all your personal belongings, you can't stop living life and worry so much about everything you own getting stolen that you miss out on the simple pleasures in life, like grilling out a nice steak!

Yet, that should not stop you from purchasing a high-temperature marker, which can withstand up to 2000 degrees Fahrenheit and makes the markings permanent when fused by heat. Simply put your last name and abbreviate your state and write your license number on your grill, lawnmower, or anything else you want to protect, and relax. At this point you have done all any prudent person could do.

Beyond marking your grill for protection, I would be remiss if I did not address a few safety concerns for those using charcoal. Do not squirt lighter fluid on coals after a flame is present on burning coals. Consider using an electric starter. Also, if you use a turkey fryer only use it outside and never on a wooden deck!

Pool Safety and Security

Between 2005 and 2007 an average of 385 children a year under the age of 15, drowned in pools and spas, and over 4,200 pool-related injuries were treated by emergency services during that same time period. Individuals who invest in having a pool or spa on their property need to be both aware and concerned about the potential hazards and do what they can to prevent accidents from happening.

First and foremost, erecting a barrier such as walls or fencing is of paramount importance in helping to limit the number of uninvited and often under-aged guests. Next, access points, such as gates, need to be self-closing and latching, making it difficult for a young child to open. All gates and windows should be wired to trigger an audible alarm if breached to alert adults that someone is in the area. Pools or spas themselves can have an alarm as well that indicates waves or the displacement of water.

When the pool or spa is not in use or out of season,

the owner should consider having either a manual or motorized cover securing the entire expanse of their pool or spa. This cover needs to be rated to hold the weight of two adults and a child.[54]

Make sure that in all situations you are in compliance with all city and county ordinances, and check with your insurance provider to make sure you are fully covered: specifically have them explain any situation where you may NOT be covered so you can avoid those circumstances from occurring.

Home Sweet Home

Obviously, if it were up to everyone, thieves would never be able to gain access to the inside of your home. In order to make this as much of a reality as possible, your best defensive action is to make sure that your doors and windows are not only properly installed and are in good working order, but that they are also further fortified to help better secure you and your family.

When it comes to doors, a solid door obviously provides greater protection than a hollow core door. A metal door allows you more protection in most cases than a wooden door.

For additional protection, some people opt to install a metal security gate or grill. Security grills also can be used to protect windows.

Note that if you have wooden doors and frames, instead of using one-inch screws opt for three-inch screws in the faceplate. The longer screws really can help fortify the strength of your door.

Having a peephole is a great idea. Make sure the field of view is at least 180 degrees. They also make a digital door peephole that runs off of a battery and allows you not only to see who is at the door, but also to record their picture on a memory card. Regardless, never feel compelled to open any door if you don't know who is on the other side! If it is important they can always come back or give you a call.

Another idea you may want to consider is adding an intercom system with your doorbell so that you can communicate with the person without having to open your door. Many intercoms now come both wired and wireless with video capabilities. The prices of these units have come down considerably.

With any serious discussion concerning doors, you need to realize that the door itself is only one aspect of this equation. The other is the security of the doorjamb or outer casing that holds your door in place. Most residential doorjambs are made of wood and are considered a weak link when it comes to security. With enough force your doorjamb will splinter easily. You also need to make sure that doors open inward so that door hinges are not exposed.

So one basic question you need to ask yourself concerning your outer perimeter protection: How easy would it be to kick in your existing doors and gain entry? The answer to this question may surprise or even shock you. In many instances it is easier and quicker to kick in a door than it is to use a key. No, I am not kidding! What may even be more shocking is that a full one-third of people fail to lock the door in the first place, so a thief does not require ANY force to gain entry!

Talk with a local locksmith and spend some time at the closest home improvement store to explore your options. With existing doors, by all means consider adding a solid metal strike box that reinforces your deadbolt to your doorframe. If you're interested in adding even more protection, I would strongly suggest you look at the product lines offered by Armor Concepts at http://www.armorconcepts.com/.

If your outer door has glass panels on the door itself, or the surrounding door casing has glass, you need to either put a security laminate on those panels or replace them with Plexiglas that is much harder to break. If not, someone could easily break the glass and reach around and unlock the door.

Some homeowners with pets have installed a door to allow their animal to go out when needed. This might have seemed like a good idea at the time, but it leaves you open for someone or something to gain access to your home from outside. I can't help but be reminded of a YouTube™ video I saw years ago of a lady in Florida calling 911 when she found an alligator in her kitchen. In doing additional research, I found that large pet doors have flap openings of 10 ⅛" X 15 ¾" and the X-Large door flap opening was a huge gap of 13 ⅜" X 23". Clearly, having an opening this large is more than just a little security threat, and anyone serious about home security should not have a pet door this large. Granted, a barking dog is a good security deterrent, but a hole in your door this large is not! If you feel like having a pet door is an absolute must, then consider the electronic version that relies on a sensor on your pet's collar that allows the door to be opened. Note, however, this feature alone still creates a risk if your pet is captured and the collar removed.

Beware also of mail slots placed in doors. A crowbar can be slid in place and used to break the door apart due to the fact that cuts in doors make them weaker and easier to gain access with a forced entry. Mail slots also give burglars the opportunity to use a device that will enable them to reach the deadbolt latch and open it.

It is your job to think about the unexpected and plan for the possible. It's honestly not that hard to critically assess your home security once you put your mind to it and are open for suggestions on ways to improve. One first critical step is to literally go outside your home and really try to think with the mind of a thief. What do you see that looks vulnerable? If you were going to break in to steal things from your own home, how would you go about doing it?

An excellent idea that adds another layer of protection to your outer perimeter door is to install a locking security storm door. In the past, most so-called storm doors were flimsy at best and were used more for ventilation and keeping bugs out than for protecting those inside from a larger threat. In the past and even now, most security doors are unattractive and look more like jail cells than something you want to put on the outside of your home. Fortunately, there is a product that is made today that gives you both security and curb appeal. That product is made by Larson: http://www.larsondoors.com

Specifically, you will want to look at their Secure Elegance® storm door. What sets this door apart from others that I have seen is that this is a full glass storm door, but it has an incredible triple latch deadbolt locking system with a reinforced frame, as well as an extra inner layer of invisible security laminate that is sandwiched in between their branded KeepSafe Glass®. While the outer glass does shatter, the laminate holds the glass in place and takes repeated hits with a blunt object. This door is in no way bulletproof, but it is extremely resistant to any type of forced entry. To be convinced that this door is for you, go to YouTube and type in Larson Secure Elegance Security and check out the video. It is worth noting that when you buy this door Larson provides a $1,000 Break-In Protection Warranty!

The Big Picture

Often forgotten areas of concern are access crawl space doors under your home, basement doors, and windows at ground level hidden away from plain view. You need to pay close attention to these areas and be brutally honest with yourself and identify all areas of vulnerability.

If you have an attached garage, is there an access point to the ceiling that also attaches to the attic that could allow entry into your home?

While it might sound a little extreme, you might consider adding a trip wire that will activate your alarm if someone cuts your phone line. Additionally, know that most security panels allow you to use cell phone technology versus having to rely on a hardwired phone line.

In addition to protecting the phone line, think about putting a lock on any outdoor panel boxes, like the breaker box to your air conditioner or your heat pump, to prevent someone on the outside from just throwing a switch and waiting for you to come out to investigate.

Locks

Your personal protection should begin with changing the locks on the doors, period. If the home is new then your builder and his crew likely had access to the key, and if you are buying a home that was previously owned then you have no idea who might have a key. Do yourself a favor and change all the locks, and remember to change the code for your garage door and alarm.

You likely have heard the security proverb, "Locks are for honest people." I think the best reason for this statement is that most doors in our homes have a latching system that keeps the door closed until someone turns the knob or pushes down on the lever to open the door. The level of security provided by the locking device on these door latches is minimal, and it relies in large part on the strength of the strike plate and what the plate itself is attached to.

Having secure locks and deadbolts is meaningless unless you make it a habit to use them! It is amazing to me the number of people who still leave their homes, cars, sheds or outbuilding doors unlocked. Reports have shown that a full one third of all home burglaries have occurred by simply opening an unlocked door and walking in!

Make sure all exterior doors on your home are locked and secure. This includes any outbuildings and garage. Finally, while attic locks are considered very rare, you might consider adding a lock to secure your attic. If you have a doorway that leads into your attic, then this door needs to be an exterior grade door and you should consider securing this door using a one sided thumb latch deadbolt. If you have a set of pull-down steps then consider using a keyed hasp lock, especially if these steps are located in a garage that would allow someone easy entry into a home from overhead. If you have an access hole instead of steps, then this, too, needs to be latched and locked.

Hiding Keys

Key rings have a tendency to become boat anchors. Do you really need all the keys on your key ring? Make sure you do not label your keys with specific names or addresses that would lead a potential thief to your home or storage unit. Also, if possible have all your keys stamped with the words "Do Not Duplicate." The fewer the keys you carry, the fewer the locks you would have to change in the event that your keys were lost or stolen.

Magnetic hide-a-key boxes were very popular at one time, and surprisingly people still use them, even though now cars have remote key fobs, push button combination locks on doors and some even OnStar™ capability to unlock doors via satellite.

I'm sure there have been millions of fake key rocks sold in America. Regardless of how covert or clever you might feel about your hidden key spot or device, the reality is it is best not to have a "hidden key" at all because of the risk it poses. Criminals know the "secret" spots and gadgets as well as you do, so don't fool yourself into thinking it is totally safe.

Resist the urge to "hide" a key outside or in the common hiding places, like under a doormat, above a door ledge and in a plant sitting next to the door. Thieves will look to find a key to open your door, so your best option is to refuse the thief that opportunity in the first place. Remember, part of the security of a key is having the right one.

Look First

We all have a bad habit of opening the door quickly when someone rings our doorbell. We might glance through a peephole if we have one, but rarely do we stop to think before opening the door. We become too relaxed if the person appears not to be a threat or is dressed like a delivery person. This is a bad habit we should all break! If you don't know who the person is or cannot see a clearly marked and recognized delivery vehicle, then it is better to not open the door, but speak to them through the door or use an intercom system.

As a last resort you can install a sliding chain lock or a door chain lock, which is a chain that fits around your door knob. You may also want to have a rubber wedge shaped door stopper on the floor next to your door that you can slide behind the door if you decide to open the door slightly to talk to someone. However, you need to realize that opening the door, no matter how small the opening, does expose you to greater danger than keeping it closed. This is also another reason to think about having an intercom system installed.

If you have not already done so, you need to install a keyed locking outer storm door with all your exterior doors! You need to develop the habit of locking and unlocking these outer storm doors as you use your regular exterior door. This truly can be your first level of defense to slow down any unwanted guests from easily rushing to enter your home. Since the vast majority of home burglaries occur by forcing entry through a front door, having a locked outer storm door only makes sense.

Beware of Scams

Door-to-door salespersons are, for the most part, a thing of the past. However, from time to time you might expect to see unexpected visitors arriving at your door step.

Some are harmless, while others might not be! Unfortunately, there is no way of telling the difference. Believe it or not, there are still people trying to go door-to-door to sell vacuums or offer carpet cleaning services, sell kitchen knives and even magazine subscriptions. I'm not including in this group the harmless, but sometimes expensive Girl Scout cookies, Boy Scout sales, or the various high school coupon book fundraisers.

Keep abreast of the various scams that are taking place in your area by contacting your local law enforcement agency. Ask them if they offer an e-mail newsletter that provides crime prevention tips as well as notification of any identified scams. Many state attorney general offices also give citizens the option of subscribing to an e-mail newsletter that helps notify people of various unscrupulous activities taking place throughout the state.

Common Ruses

Someone knocks on your door to tell you they have just hit your car. Tell the person that you are going to call the police and wait until they arrive before you go out to investigate. Someone knocks on your door and they tell you their car is broken down or they have a flat tire. Tell them you will be glad to call someone for them and ask for the number, but tell them this is all you can offer.

A fake flower delivery can be tempting. However, instead of opening the door, tell the delivery person to put the flowers down and you will get them later. If they say you must sign, keep the door closed and ask for the florist's name and phone number. Tell them you have to call first to make sure the delivery is a legitimate one.

If you have someone telling you there is a gas leak in the area and they need to check your home, do not let them in before calling your utility company to verify this is true.

Your purse goes missing at a store, and you are called and informed that it has been found and you need to return to the store to claim it. First, get the person's name and look up the store phone number and call back to verify this is true. It could be that the person who took your purse looked at your driver's license and has driven to your home and is waiting outside for you to leave so they can break in!

Theft can happen at any time, and often when you least expect it. One example is when a visitor to your yard sale asks to use your bathroom. Large neighborhood Christmas parties have even been known to attract well-dressed, friendly strangers looking for something to quickly steal, and I don't mean a bite to eat or a mixed drink.

Anytime anyone you do not know very well or a friend of a friend comes inside your home for any reason, be suspect and careful!

The Invited Stranger

It does not matter if you are a homeowner or a renter – from time to time you have to invite strangers into your home. This might be a plumber, electrician or maybe even a yard guy asking to use your bathroom. Anytime anyone you really don't know enters your home you are putting yourself at some risk. If you know in advance that service work is going to be done, you need to make sure keys as well as paperwork with sensitive information or other valuable items that could easily be slipped in a pocket or purse are put away and secure. This includes your daily calendar! No stranger should know the schedule of when you will be away from home.

If you have someone that comes in to clean your home, you need to make sure a criminal records check is done on that individual. You may also want to consider having a locked closet or cabinet for valuables and sensitive information you want to keep secure.

Keeping You Secure

All homes should have deadbolts on exterior doors, and you should also consider having non-keyed deadbolts on inner doors, such as bedrooms. The strongest inner door should be made of solid wood or steel, versus the normal hollow core door found in most homes. Interior deadbolts can provide you with an extra layer of security. If an intruder enters your home and you are not able to flee, you can lock an interior door to give you time to try to call for help or find a defensive weapon. Instead of having the standard strike plate, you should consider replacing each door plate with the full metal strike box that has multiple anchor points into your door frame, the same as with your exterior doors.

When looking for locks, do your own research to see what fits your budget, then buy the highest grade of lock you can comfortably afford. Remember to talk to a locksmith in your area and ask them what lock he uses on his home. If pushed to make one recommendation, and money were no object, the best lock to use would be a lock made by Abloy® called the Protec2 which uses a disc locking system, making it very difficult to pick. With that said, most people breaking into homes are not professionals, but are criminals looking for opportunity – they prefer to kick in doors rather than picking the lock.

Where Did I Put My Keys?

If you only focus on the type of door or lock then you might be missing a critical part of securing your entryways. You also need to know who has the keys! The strongest door in the world will not keep a person out if they have the key. How many keys do you have floating around? Does your neighbor have a key to your house in case you get locked out? Do they secure the key, or is it tagged with your name on it and laying in plain view?

Many people keep their car and house keys in a cabinet or drawer near the door leading to the garage for convenience. It may be better to keep them in a locked key cabinet or in a less-obvious place, like in a bowl in the refrigerator. Be sure not to put electronic key fobs in the refrigerator. Try to think convenient but not obvious. As crazy as it may sound, there are stories of burglars who not only broke into the person's home – but loaded up the family car in the garage with their new found loot!

Windows and Glass

A big challenge most homeowners face is that of making sure windows and, more importantly, patio doors or French style doors are secure. The challenge for both is the large surface area of glass that can, in most instances, be easily broken.

Most window and door glass in homes today is tempered glass, like that used in automobiles. This is a type of safety glass that is both stronger than regular plate glass and has the added bonus that if it breaks it shatters into small pebbles versus leaving sharp edges.

There are several extra methods of protection for windows. One method that is not used often today involves having your outside screen panel alarmed. The panel still allows a breeze to pass through, but if the screen is cut or removed the alarm activates. These panels either connect to your home alarm or have a built-in, stand-alone alarm.

Another inexpensive option is to cut a wooden dowel rod or a piece of PVC pipe and place this in the window tracking to help secure the window sash in position if someone were to break out a window. Make sure the rod or pipe is snug in place and secure it with Velcro® if needed.

For sliding glass doors, consider using a charley bar or a dowel rod to keep the door in place. Also, as a test, lift up on the door from the outside and make sure it cannot be easily removed from the track. If it can, you might need to add screws in the top part of the tracking to prevent removal.

If you are fond of leaving your windows open at night for ventilation, then you need to make sure that you have a window stop in place that only allows a small gap in height to occur to prevent unauthorized entry. It is important to check to make sure that all windows freely open and close, especially in rooms that have been recently painted. Sealed windows can create a deadly fire hazard!

Another added layer of protection which, in my opinion, is well worth the money is adding a clear security laminate to all windows and large glass doors and panels, especially at the ground level of your home. I recommend you research and go online to find the nearest 3M™ dealer that specializes in safety and security window films, specifically the "3M™ Impact Protection Attachment Systems."

Again, look online at various videos of people breaking this glass with the laminate attached. One video I saw was from an actual security camera footage that showed two criminals in action. You can't help but be extremely impressed with this product.

French style glass doors are extremely hard to secure, but using keyed deadbolts and sliding rods at both the top and bottom of the door help provide additional strength to the door itself. It goes without saying that you need laminated glass to make it more difficult to gain entry.

The Weakest Link

If you have a window air conditioning unit, this too needs to be secured with brackets – not only to support the unit itself, but also to make it harder to move to gain entry. Make sure the window is locked in place as much as possible to prevent a burglar from sliding the window up and down. A cheap, battery-operated magnetic window sensor contact is something you can easily install that will create noise to alert you if someone is trying to gain entry. It also has the potential to scare someone away.

In some cases, if you have a sliding glass window that you do not use, you may want to consider replacing it with a solid glass block or a solid plastic block window that looks like glass. Both are an excellent source of diffused light, but they also provide a great deal of protection.

CHAPTER ELEVEN

When You Were Away

For a moment I'd like you read and think about the following scenario:

A thief is riding in your neighborhood at 10 a.m. in an unmarked van. It is recycle day; he stops down the road and retrieves an empty cardboard box from a home a block over from your house. He places a screwdriver and a pillowcase inside. He closes the lid of the box, rejoins the label and then puts clear tape on the box and makes sure the label is showing.

He arrives at your home and notices no cars are in the driveway. He is dressed in a brown shirt and pants. He is carrying a clipboard with a paper attached with signatures and a pen. With box in hand, he slips on a pair of sunglasses and walks to your door and rings your doorbell to see if anyone will answer the door. If someone does he pretends to be at the wrong address. But since no one is home, he continues.

Since it is a little after 10 in the morning on Wednesday, everyone in your neighborhood is at work except Mrs. Patterson, who lives five doors down. Very few cars are parked in driveways up and down your street. Unfortunately, you were running late for work this morning and forgot to turn on your alarm system.

Since no one appears to be home, the thief decides to go around to the back of your home. He sees a large glass patio door. He looks inside and sees a nice large flat screen TV in your den. He puts on his gloves and grabs his screwdriver from the fake package and makes his first attempt in trying to pry the door open. It is locked tightly, so he grabs a rock from your patio garden and tosses it through the patio door. The safety glass shatters into a million pieces and he punches enough glass out to reach in and unlock the door.

No alarm sounds; he glances at his watch and feels confident that he has plenty of time to look around.

He steps in your den and looks for anything of value. He quickly unhooks your TV and places it by the door. A set of silver candlesticks from the mantle is removed and placed inside the pillowcase, along with a few other items from a bookshelf that look interesting. In a scan of the kitchen, he spots a laptop computer on the kitchen countertop that is also placed in the pillowcase. A fast dash is then made to the bedrooms upstairs. He passes your child's bedroom and goes straight to the master bedroom. Bedside table drawers are dumped on the bed, as well as the contents of the jewelry box from your dresser. Anything that looks valuable is taken and placed into the pillowcase.

Quickly looking at his watch, he sees that ten minutes have elapsed. He realizes it's time to go. He grabs the TV and carries it to the van. Opening the back doors, he gently places the TV on a blanket and shuts the doors quickly. He goes back to the patio door and grabs the box, clipboard, and pillowcase. He makes his way back to the van and leaves your neighborhood.

He then heads back to his house only a few miles away to drop off the pillowcase. On his way he drives by an area known for selling and buying drugs and stops to talk to a group of guys he knows hanging out on the corner. He offers them a nice flat screen TV for $50 and finds a buyer. Satisfied for now, he decides it is time to go to lunch!

While this story is fictional, it does give you a true picture of what can and often does happen.

Who is Mr. Burglar?

Research shows that over 60 percent of the home burglaries in the United States happen between the hours of 10 a.m. and 3 p.m. While crime obviously happens year round, a spike in burglaries tends to occur during the months of July and August when people are away from their homes for longer periods of time for summer vacations.

The ones most committing these offenses are males under twenty-five-years-old who live only few miles away from the home they burglarize. The most common entry point for a break-in is through the front door. Entry is gained by kicking open the door with the doorjamb failing. The next two common entry points are through a first floor window or by using a back door. Generally, the first room targeted is the master bedroom.

The total amount of time spent looking in your home is from eight to twelve minutes.

Hidden in Plain Sight

Today people have devised all types of ingenious ways to create "a safe" that goes beyond the conventional steel box with a lock on it. It makes sense for everyone to consider either purchasing or building your own diversion safe and even to have a few placed in different areas of your home. These "safes" are made from common everyday items or food containers, like a potato chip can, or built into items like mantel clocks. One inexpensive diversion item is a woman's black blouse that has nine clear zipper pockets. It can be hung on a hanger in your closet next to other clothes and no one can tell the difference.

Obviously, these safes are not meant to be objects that you would relate to security devices, but items that blend in with the environment. Few criminals breaking into a home would look in the bathroom beside the toilet at a canister that has a roll of toilet paper on top. Likewise, a criminal is less likely to take the time to go through your freezer and open what looks to be a box of frozen spinach to find your extra cash.

Another unique idea that goes beyond the conventional safe is an overhead vault system that you can find online at http://www.overheadvault.com. This would work well in a crawl space or attic.

I recommend you do a lot of research on your own and think about the different applications for using safes like these to hide small items, like car keys or extra garage remote controls. There is no reason to keep you from having hidden compartments or cubbyholes in unexpected places as well. These can be excellent options to hide the things you don't want discovered instantly if someone breaks into your home.

The real key in all of this is to make it as difficult as possible for the bad guy, but still maintain a livable home environment, so it is a win/win situation. I realize this is a tough balancing act, but this is a goal to keep in mind regardless. Remember that once a thief enters your home he or she is going to be looking for what can grabbed quickly and what might sell fast on the street. Any electronics or anything gold or silver will be looked at closely.

The following are just a few websites that will help you to start opening your mind to the different possibilities of places you can hide items in plain sight:

http://covertfurniture.com
http://secretcompartmentfurniture.com
http://www.greatstuff.com/furniture.html
http://www.hiddensafes.com/index.htm
http://bedgunsafe.com/

Safes: Real or Imagined Protection?

In discussing the topic of safes you really need to step back and first determine what you are ultimately trying to accomplish. Most people think of a safe for either security protection or fire protection, or both.

If you are in the market for a safe, it is not uncommon to find yourself feeling both confused and overwhelmed. A lot of what you find on the Internet is just hype by those pushing a specific product. Most don't give you the tools you need to accurately measure the effectiveness of their product in comparison to others. In the United States we have an independent organization known as Underwriter Laboratories (UL).

This organization has created the standards for the industry to go by. Furthermore, it is also the agency that conducts the actual test to see that the specific safe in question actually meets that standard.

As in many cases, what generally starts out as a discussion concerning security ends up being a real conversation about price and what you can afford to purchase. A Toyota and a BMW are both cars. Both are likely to get you to your destination, so only you can determine if the differences in safety and luxury are worth the price you have to pay.

The price of a safe will vary depending on many factors, such as size, weight and overall protection. You will need to first determine where the safe will be kept.

How Important Are The Valuables You Want To Protect?

Unfortunately, many of the safes sold today are made as cheaply as possible overseas to be sold to the general public through retail merchant chains. The stores research the price point the consumer is willing to pay on a certain item. So the driving factor in making most mass-produced safes is to create a product within a certain dollar range versus focusing on the actual ability to provide security protection.

Many in the industry would tell you it is a race to the bottom to determine who can provide the product the cheapest.

This trend can be devastating to the homeowner. In effect, you may be thinking you are buying one thing only to find out you have purchased another.

Fire Protection or Burglary

Most people fail to realize that a safe built for fire protection offers little to no burglary protection. It can be confusing, so it is important that you do carefully inspect and research what you are thinking about buying and not just buy something because it looks good! If you are fortunate to locate an actual showroom of a company that sells safes, ignore the shiny outside finish, graphics and even the brand name, or the set of rods that crank and anchor into the inner door. Instead, pay close attention to the overall construction of both the body and door to the safe.

Choosing to purchase a safe needs to be done as part of your overall security plan – not your only means of protecting your valuables. You need to remember that most individuals who commit home burglaries do so quickly and do not spend a lot of time in the residence. A decent safe, properly secured, should be able to thwart their attack.

Some burglary safes do have a fireboard, i.e. drywall, in them or are made of a composite material that offers some fire protection, but generally this offers limited protection. It is also important to understand that when a safe has a layer of drywall in it, the moisture in the material vaporizes and turns into steam when heated. So if you store items like important papers, old photos or firearms in your safe, these can easily be destroyed in the event of a fire. You need to think not only how the contents of your safe will fare against the heat of a fire, but also whether it can withstand the water that might be applied to extinguish the flame.

One easy way to resolve this problem is to invest in a product called SureSeal™ by FireKing™. This product comes in various sizes and is basically a box that has a special seal which offers a fireproof rating and is waterproof. This is perfect to fit inside any safe allowing you to protect important papers or firearms.

Security Safes

A starting point for a basic security safe is one that carries the UL Residential Security Container (RSC) B Rating. What this means is that the container can withstand five minutes of tools being applied against the door and has a UL Group 2M lock. The tools used in this test are standard household tools, like a crowbar or a drill. The door of the safe should have at least a half-inch steel door and a quarter-inch steel body. The next step up is a C Rated safe that has a one-inch thick door with a half-inch steel body. Be aware that many safe manufacturers have on the interior of the safe door a thick hollow metal box that basically hides the gears and locking bolts. At first glance this appears impressive, but it offers little real protection. Thick bolts do not always mean security; look inside to see if the metal that throws those bolts locked is a thin or a solid metal rod.

The next level of safe are those advertised as having a TL-15 rating, which identifies that fifteen minutes is the net time someone applies tools to the safe door with an additional eight minutes working on the body of the safe. The tools used are those used by the professional locksmiths and professional thieves. These may include tungsten-carbide drill bits in high-speed drills, as well as grinding tools. Jewelers, as well as serious collectors of high-value items, would likely choose this type of safe or one rated at a higher level. If you are serious about protection, owning at least a TL-15 should be the starting point!

A TL-30 rated safe, or one that offers thirty minutes of protection, can withstand more abuse than a TL-15 rated safe, and a TL-60 can withstand attacks longer than a TL-30. Another variation you will see is the abbreviation X6. This typically applies to a TL30-X6 or TL60-X6. What this means is that not only the safe door can withstand the attack for thirty or sixty minutes, but all sides of the safe are protected as well.

Having a UL Burglar rated safe is important, not only for protection but also if you plan on insuring the contents. The value of the items you can insure in a safe increases as the level of protection increases. Insurance companies vary on the amount that you can insure, but generally a TL-15 safe with an alarm system can have contents covered for as much as $200,000. A TL-30 safe with an alarm system in place can be insured for as much as $375,000.

The next category UL assigns a lettering and number code are for a special class of safes known as a TRTL-30 or TRTL-60, which means the combination safe and group 2M lock can withstand both handheld, electric operating tools as well as oxy-fuel welding and cutting torch for either thirty or sixty minutes respectively. Finally, the highest rating is Class TXTL-60, which meets the prior standard but goes further to be able to withstand a certain amount of high explosives as well. Generally only government agencies or large corporations have the ability to afford these types of safes or really need this type of protection. Again, the X6 abbreviation can also be used, noting that protection is on all sides of the safe.

It is extremely important to note that many people are confused by what appears to be the short duration of times given in the safe rating system. This time does NOT represent the time it took to actually break into the safe, but ONLY the amount of time tools were applied!

One of the best websites I found that helps give you a real in-depth education about safes comes from a company called C.E. Safe. They can be found online at http://cesafes.com.

Regardless of how big and heavy your safe might be, unless your home was built around your safe, it MUST be bolted and secured to the floor or to the wall.

Beware of Dog!

Place on your window or door and/or fence a sign stating "Beware of Dog!" Second, adopt your own electronic Watch Dog Rex Plus® from the Safety Technology International: http://www.sti-usa.com. This device has motion-sensing technology that actually penetrates through doors and even walls to detect movement up to twenty-five feet away. It takes less than five minutes to set and it is portable as well.

There are other products that utilize a pressure sensitive mat that, when activated, causes the sound of a dog barking to begin. For extra effect, place a large dog bowl outside your door.

CHAPTER TWELVE

Security Systems –
The Electronic Watchman

By far one of the most widely used tools for theft protection is an alarm system.

At one time having an alarm system was a considerable deterrent. Alarms are still generally effective, but they remain mostly a reactive tool.

Years ago security alarms were expensive and only a few residents had them. As the market changed, companies realized that the money was not just made in selling the alarm hardware, but by counting on the recurring revenue they would receive in a monitoring service agreement. Some companies will practically give you a basic alarm system for the ability to lock you into a long-term monitoring contract.

In order to make you feel better about purchasing a home security system, companies also try to entice you with options. Some security panels will also monitor for fire protection that might include smoke and/or carbon monoxide detection, as well as rapid-rise heat detection. There is a wide array of sensors that alarm panels use, beyond the simple door or window contacts.

These include glass break detection, shock or vibration sensors, and the detection of motion or even weight with the use of pressure pads that can be placed on stair steps. Other security panels may monitor possible water flow detected from a burst pipe from thawing after freezing, or potential flooding of a basement in the event a sump pump fails, a drain backs up or a water heater leaks.

Furthermore, some systems allow you to turn on and off various lights or appliances and set your thermostat, as well as connect you through video monitoring to see what is happening in real time using your smart phone or computer.

Another common feature gives you the ability to set a hostage or panic code. This code allows for the individuals to "disarm" the system so the horn or siren does not sound, but instead sends a silent alarm to the security company to notify the police that a potential hostage situation is occurring.

Keep in mind that when most people purchase a security system they are not really thinking about how reliable the equipment might be, or about all of the features the alarm system offers. They are only really focused on the response time from law enforcement, which is something the alarm company has no control over.

Questions to Ask

If you are thinking about installing a security system, ask plenty of questions to the salesman who will train you and your family to operate the system. Ask for the references of other customers who currently use the alarm system you are thinking about installing to see if they have had any difficulty with the system. Find out what type of customer and/or technical service is offered after the sale and what the cost is for a service call.

When you design your alarm system determine what areas are NOT covered. Will the alarm system cover an outbuilding like a storage shed or an unattached garage? If there is a power outage, does your system have a battery backup, and if so how long does this last? How often will the main battery, as well as any sensor batteries, need to be replaced and at what cost? Can additional sensors be added later if you want to expand your coverage? What type of warranty does your system have? Is it covered in the event of a power surge or lightning strike? Who will actually install the system – the company selling the system to you or outside contract installers? Are permits needed? If your alarm system is monitored, how are false alarms handled, and how do you set up passwords and change who you want to be contacted if an alarm does sound? Does the system do self-testing? Lastly, who do I call if I have any additional questions or concerns?

Companies that sell security systems are required by law in most states to call the owner first if an alarm is activated, to make sure it is not a false alarm, before calling law enforcement. Yet, the perception most people have when the alarm sounds is that somehow law enforcement knows there is a problem and will arrive instantly. Unfortunately, this is not true in most cases!

Types of Systems

There are two basic types of security alarm systems. One is a hardwired system where all of the alarm sensors tie directly into the main control panel. The second is a wireless system that generally uses battery-powered sensors that communicate remotely to the control panel. Many systems also combine the use of both hardwired and wireless sensors in designing a system. Further systems also can use a hardwired telephone line or cell phone technology to communicate to an alarm monitoring service.

You first need to determine the purpose for installing a security system and what you are trying to accomplish. Do you want to design a system mainly for the protection of your valuables while you are away, or are you mostly concerned about your personal safety? Many people want both!

The most basic system will have at least one panel located inside your home that arms and disarms the system. It is safer to have several control panels, with one being by the door you use most to leave and enter your home, and one panel inside your master bedroom. At night, after locking all exterior doors, you should also be able to lock your master bedroom door and arm your system.

You should protect ALL exterior doors! This should include the door that connects to your garage, as well as your basement and an entry door from outside into the garage or basement. Keep in mind that exterior grade doors should be used for your garage and basement, not hollow core interior doors. Don't forget to include any crawl space access doors that go under your home and, if possible, protect the doors that secure any outbuildings, like storage sheds.

There is a wide array of intruder detection devices that can affix to windows and doors. The following is a list of some of these devices: magnetic contact switches, shock or seismic sensors, pressure detection sensors, sensors that use a beam of light, fiber-optic mesh and glass break detectors. Keep in mind there are also devices you can employ that can detect movement, heat or sound.

When your alarm system is programmed, make sure each alarm sensor is connected to a separate zone. This is extremely important because, when an alarm is activated, the monitoring company needs to be able to tell the person or persons they notify where the source of the potential break-in was first identified.

Your basic alarm system should have at least one glass break detector and a smoke detector that activates your alarm in the event of a fire. Finally, the alarm should have an internal and external LOUD alarm speaker or horn, and you should have your system monitored by a professional monitoring service.

**Note that if you use magnetic door contacts, make sure the contact switch is located at the bottom of the door versus the top. Burglars have been known to cut open doors using a battery-operated circular saw and swing open the bottom to avoid triggering the alarm.

Again, realize that when you are shopping for an alarm system you will likely be quoted the price for a basic system that includes only a certain number of sensors that may or may not do an adequate job of protecting your property. Items like panic buttons, rapid rise heat detection systems, and remote video capabilities are all possibilities, but may not be offered in a basic package.

Don't feel pressured into buying something you don't want or need just because it is part of the package. There is normally more than one company that sells alarms in your area. Beyond looking in your phone book, call your local law enforcement agency and ask to speak to the officer who is in charge of crime prevention and ask them if they have a list of alarm companies. Ask about their policies concerning responding to alarms. Some agencies require the homeowner to pay a fee to register the alarm system so they can receive the department's policy on responding to false calls and possible fines that may be imposed.

You SHOULD arm your alarm system when you are AWAY as well as when you are at HOME. Alarm systems have designated home and away modes for a purpose! At the very least, most alarm systems also have a "chime mode" that you can set to alert you when a door has been opened.

Simply stated: Failing to utilize the alarm as it was designed lessens the capability of its effectiveness as a tool for your protection. Don't lull yourself into thinking you only need to arm the system when you are out of town. Your simple run to the store offers a thief plenty of time to smash and grab. Remember, most break-ins happen during the daytime.

False Alarm

A quick read on the Internet reveals that 95 percent to 98 percent of all alarm activations are false. Alarm calls in most areas of the country are considered low priority calls by law enforcement. Response times can be slow or, in some jurisdictions, law enforcement does not respond at all! It is worth noting that many jurisdictions that respond to alarm activations have enacted local ordinances that will fine the homeowner if law enforcement is asked to respond to a certain number of false alarm activations.

Initially, when an alarm call is reported to law enforcement the dispatcher will often check records to determine if the location has a history of false alarm activity. Likewise during thunderstorms and bad weather, when alarm activations are more frequent and response times can be even slower.

Before investing a large amount of money into a security system, you need to do your own research and again contact your local law enforcement to see what their policy is concerning responding to alarm activations. You need to realize that you and you alone are responsible for your personal security. You cannot and should not count on someone else coming to your rescue, as much as you would like to think this might happen. It is a simple fact that law enforcement cannot be everywhere at one time, and criminals know more than most what the response time might be if an alarm is activated.

Let me be clear. I am a firm believer that every home should have an alarm system and that the alarm should be loud and audible with a horn and/or voice command that can be heard both inside and outside the home. However, I think it is important that you do not have a false sense of security simply because you have installed a basic security system. Remember, security alarms provide only "passive protection," which is a reactionary tool.

Cameras and DVR

Home security cameras have come a long way in a short amount of time. Not that long ago, the typical cameras you were able to purchase were expensive and very large, and they did not really provide a clear image. Today, however, everything has changed, as has the ability to record what a camera sees and how to view those images.

Much like alarms, having a camera with the ability to record what it sees will not necessarily prevent a crime from happening, but it can definitely be a deterrent. It also greatly enhances the ability to apprehend any suspect.

If you are serious about security, then you should consider a professionally installed camera and DVR or digital video recording system for your home, period! I know many folks might want to opt for the "do-it-yourself kits" that are sold practically everywhere, but in my opinion you ultimately get what you pay for.

Most people want excellent resolution on the cameras as well as the capability to view what your camera sees in low light at nighttime. Second, you want to be able to have real-time recording and have those images stored retrieved later if any event occurs. Remote monitoring has now become a reality with smart phones, and the prices for all of this technology have come down so much it puts it within the budget of more people than ever before.

Designing a security camera and recording system for you and your home or office is something that should not be done quickly. You should really take your time and think about your current needs and even additional needs you might have later. One of the biggest mistakes most people make is buying a boxed, all-in-one camera system that is too small or does not have the right type or number of cameras.

Also, when thinking of a security camera system you have to determine if a hardwired system or a wireless system best fits your needs. With either option, a long-term power source will be needed. Battery operated cameras never last long enough and will cause you to miss something you might later wish was recorded.

Additional Camera & DVR Questions to Consider

You need to first determine what you want to see and why you want to see it. How many cameras do you need now? Does the system have the capability to add cameras later? One mistake that happens frequently is that people purchase a system that is maxed out to start. Inevitably in the future another camera will need to be added, and the system either cannot support the new camera or makes it more costly to do so.

Do you want to record the images shown, or are you just using the video from the camera or cameras to monitor what is currently taking place? Are the camera or cameras you plan on using internal, which are typically not waterproof, or do you want external cameras that may be water resistant or waterproof? How many monitors do you want to have in place, and where you do want those monitors to be located? Will the viewing be split screen so you see all the cameras at one time? Do you want video and audio capability or is just video sufficient? How important is viewing at night?

Most cameras that claim to have the capability of being "low lux," i.e. low light cameras, even those with a built-in infrared light source, typically do not provide a very clear picture at night when little ambient light is present. If you do not have an adequate light source you may have to add what is known as infrared illuminators or have a camera with this feature built in. Note, however, that this will require additional power usage than for regular non-infrared cameras. The idea is that, by using an ultraviolet light source transmitted through LED lights, you will be able to view what you are looking at more clearly in low light situations. However, this ability can be greatly diminished when viewing certain scenes that include surfaces like grass, brick or blacktop. All of these surfaces absorb, rather than reflect light, which hinders the camera's field of view. Before you purchase any camera system it is imperative that you know both the day and night capability of the cameras you will be using.

Today the best civilian camera you can purchase uses the technology that was originally developed for the US military, which takes advantage of light amplification. By choosing to use this type of camera you will not have any scene reflective issues that impede your view, and the clarity of view you have in relation to distance should be the same during day and night.

Most security cameras have a fixed lens, which means the focal point of what the camera can view is set and you cannot zoom in or out. With this being the case, it is important to determine what you expect your field of view to be when selecting a camera. The higher the millimeter of the lens, the more narrow the view. A 3.0 mm camera lens allows someone to see an approximately 127-degree field of view. A 6.0 mm lens has an approximate 78-degree field and view and, lastly, a 12 mm lens has a 28-degree field of view. Another factor to determine in advance is how long you want to be able to store the images recorded. Do you want to view those images remotely? If so, make sure the system has this capability. It's important to note that cameras using high definition lenses will require more hard drive storage space for your DVR. Make sure you know in advance before purchasing any system how long video images can be stored.

Clearly, with this information as a backdrop you can see the need for sitting down one-on-one with a security video specialist to help you design the best system for your specific application. Technology is changing so rapidly that literally the best camera system and DVR you choose today for your application will likely be considered nearly obsolete in a year or less.

The Life-Saving Moment

When an alarm is activated while you are at home, what is your next step?

One of the most critical aspects of having a security system – and something that families rarely discuss – is what everyone is supposed to do when an alarm is activated. Do you have a plan in place that everyone in your family will follow? Further, have you practiced your plan? Unfortunately, most people don't like to or want to think about this, but you should be prepared.

Questions to Ponder

What would you do if you drove into your driveway and saw the front door of your home kicked open? Your response should be to leave and call law enforcement! NEVER go in the home until after law enforcement has searched the house to make sure no one is inside.

If your security alarm goes off and you are home what are you going to do? If you think it is a good idea to play detective and go looking for trouble then, in my opinion, you have made the wrong choice. No possession is worth losing your life over!

Keep Bedside

Keep a list of emergency numbers close by each phone. Make sure you include both the emergency and non-emergency numbers for your local law enforcement as well as your local fire department. Also have the number for the poison control center. The United States National Poison Control Hotline phone number is 800-222-1222.

If you wear glasses have them by your bed so, in the event you hear a bump in the night, you won't need to be bothered by looking for your glasses. Keep a cell phone turned on by your bed regardless if you have a landline running to your home. The reason is simple – a hardwired line can be cut or, even easier, a phone extension in another room can be taken off the hook to make your phone inoperable.

Note that even old cell phones that are no longer connected to a paid cell service still allow you to call 911! It is a good idea to keep those old phones charged and in any location you might be using as a safe room.

Some people also have under their bed an extra set of clothes or a "go bag" to grab if they have to exit their home in an emergency. If you choose to do this, you should also have a copy of your important papers in this bag to take with you.

All this might sound melodramatic, but planning ahead could save your life. It is well worth the effort now to discuss with every member of your family the steps everyone should take in the event of something unexpected happening, like a home break-in. Remember, the best defense is a good offense!

CHAPTER THIRTEEN

Fire Safety and Protection

If you have a fire, or a suspected fire, in your home, what should you do? You should have an escape plan to get out! This plan needs to be known by everyone living in your house, including small children, and you should practice this plan at least twice a year during both daylight and night hours. Your fire plan should include not just how to get out, but where to meet after you escape.

Fire extinguishers need to be in at least three areas of your home. First, make sure you have a fire extinguisher accessible in your kitchen. Next make sure you have one in your master bedroom that is not buried in a closet or dresser drawer. Lastly, place a fire extinguisher in your garage. Remember, the time to learn how to use a fire extinguisher is not when you need it, but before. Also note that all fire extinguishers need to be checked regularly to make sure they are fully charged.

Kitchen Fires

It is easy to become terrified if you walk into your kitchen and discover that the pot or pan you left only for a second is now on fire. What should you do? If the flames are not out of control, you can try to fight the fire with either a fire extinguisher or a box of baking soda; placing a lid on the flame to smother the fire is also an option. However, you might also want to consider having a fire blanket available. These are more commonly found in Europe, but are becoming more popular in the United States. You will find many suppliers, but one company that stands out is called Safeti First™. They offer a one-time use fire blanket that measures 39" X 39." To use it, you simply pull it out from the case and place the blanket over an open flame to smother a small fire, like a common kitchen grease fire. Once the blanket is secure, turn off the heat and let it sit. The blanket comes in a compact case that can be mounted inside a kitchen cabinet and is made of a 100% woven glass fabric that is fireproof up to 1020 degrees Fahrenheit.

Another device that is specifically geared toward the kitchen grease fire is, basically, a small can that attaches above your stove and/or below your microwave over the stove. This ingenious device has a heat sensitive fuse that pops when burned, releasing the contents of the can to help smother the fire. The device is called Stovetop Firestop®, http://www.stovetopfirestop.com, and sells through a chain of national distributors.

Have a Fire Plan

Small flames can become major fires in as little as thirty seconds! With that in mind, you need to literally map out each room of your home on paper and make sure you can identify at least two ways out. Likewise, having a fire plan should not be limited to just your home, but your workplace as well.

This means making sure that you can open and close both windows and doors with ease.

Before opening any door, feel the door to see if it feels hot. If it does, do not open it! If the room is full of smoke you should crawl low on the floor in your escape. If your home has a second floor then you need to think about buying a UL-tested fire escape ladder. One brand to consider is The QuickEscape™ Emergency Escape Ladder that can be found online at http://boldindustries. com. This ladder comes in either twelve or twenty foot lengths and supports a thousand pounds of weight. The ladder also features standoffs on the rungs that keep the ladder away from the wall to help stabilize the ladder during your descent.

According to the U.S. Fire Administration (USFA), "Electrical fires in our homes claim the lives of 280 Americans each year and injure 1,000 more. Some of these fires are caused by electrical system failures, but many more are caused by incorrectly installed wiring and overloaded circuits and extension cords. During a typical year, home electrical problems account for 26,100 fires and $1 billion in property losses. About half of all residential electrical fires involve electrical wiring."[55]

Home Fire Prevention Tips
Small things can become big things, especially when it comes to preventing a fire and keeping you

and your home safe. Look at all toxic chemicals you have, both in your kitchen and garage, and ask yourself if they are really needed. You also might have a growing collection of items that need to be thrown away. Your attic and garage should not be stuffed with stacks of old newspapers, bills or magazines; this is nothing but an accident waiting to happen. Purge yourself of excess paper now! Also, make sure your garage does not have piles of sawdust or oily rags lying about. Do not store large quantities of gas or propane tanks in your garage either. Water heaters, especially gas ones, should be strapped securely to a wall. Think about buying a cheap, battery-operated water detection device that you can place inside the drip pan of your hot water heater and the overflow pan for your air conditioner, especially if the unit is located in your attic. This cheap device could end up saving you a bundle of money in the long run.

Think about installing a carbon monoxide detector in your home, as well as in your garage, especially if you use your chimney or space heater on a regular basis or have gas appliances. Don't smoke in bed, EVER! If your panel box is constantly tripping a breaker, then have a licensed electrician identify the issue and get it resolved. Get serious and look around your home to make sure you are not using an excessive number of extension cords or that you have not overloaded wall sockets. Change Christmas lights out to the newer LED lights that are safer and not as hot. Beware of using cheap electric candles in your windows and do not leave a room unattended with open flame candles or incense burning.

A real danger can occur by using a three-prong plug converter, which causes the circuit to not be properly grounded. Additional risks occur when we put a higher wattage bulb into a socket that is only rated for a lower voltage.

Finally, pay close attention to where electric items are in relation to water sources, specifically your hair dryer, electric razor or electric radio. If you drop these items in a sink of water or tub, even if they are not turned on, do not reach in to retrieve them without first unplugging them from the wall.

Fireplaces and Wood Stoves

The U.S. Fire Administration (USFA) states: "More than one-third of Americans use fireplaces, wood stoves and other fuel-fired appliances as primary heat sources in their homes. Unfortunately, many people are unaware of the fire risks when heating with wood and solid fuels. Heating fires account for 36 percent of residential home fires in rural areas every year. Often these fires are due to creosote buildup in chimneys and stovepipes. All home heating systems require regular maintenance to function safely and efficiently."[56]

When was the last time you had your chimney inspected for damage or possible blockage, and when was the last time it was cleaned? You might want to start by looking in your local phone book under chimney sweep to find a qualified professional in your area that can inspect as well as clean fireplaces and wood stoves. You also could contact your local fire department to see if they have a list of people in the area.

In addition to a professional inspection, not in the place of one, there are several off-the-shelf products you can purchase that can help you keep your chimney clean of creosote buildup. The first product is called the Creosote Sweeping Log, or CSL for short: http://cleanyourchimney.com. A second product is the Creosote Conditioner Stick made by the Imperial Company: http://www.imperialgroup.ca/index.cfm

As you consider your chimney inspection, don't forget about the top part of your chimney. The HY-C Company Inc.: http://www.hyccompany.com/ offers several types of chimney covers, as well as animal control screens for your fireplace. The chimney cap is important because it not only keeps birds and other animals out of your chimney, but also protects against debris like twigs from falling into your chimney. A cap also gives added protection from rainwater and snow to the lining of your chimney.

Clothes Dryer Fires

According to the U.S. Fire Administration, "An estimated 2,900 clothes dryer fires in residential buildings are reported to U.S. fire departments each year and cause an estimated 5 deaths, 100 injuries, and $35 million in property loss."[57]

When was the last time you checked your dryer's lint trap? Since most dryers are vented to the outside, you need to take extra care in making sure the vent system is properly operating and not clogged. If it is taking longer to dry those clothes than it once did, then lint build-up may be causing the problem.

Lint from clothing cannot only clog the piping system inside your home, but animals from the outside, like birds, squirrels and mice, have been known to crawl in and build nests that block the flow of air. This creates a real hazard. The Imperial Manufacturing Group at http://www.imperialgroup.ca has a product called the Universal Pest Guard that you can purchase at most home improvement stores that installs over either your three or four-inch dryer or bathroom fan exhaust vent to help protect you from birds or other rodents.

Become As Lint Free As Possible

A simple and effective way to help clean your dryer vent is to first unplug the dryer, then vacuum all the places you can reach to remove any lint build-up. Next, unhook the flex pipe from the back of your dryer and use an electric leaf blower to force the lint out the pipe. Make sure you wrap a towel around the flex pipe before you turn on the blower, and be sure that outside the vent is clear of all the excess debris before operating your dryer.

The Smell of Danger – Smoke Detection

"According to the National Fire Protection Association, almost two-thirds of home fire deaths resulted from fires in properties without working smoke alarms.

A working smoke alarm significantly increases your chances of surviving a deadly home fire."[58]

Everyone should at least make a point to change the battery in your smoke detector annually or purchase the detector with 10-year lithium batteries. Also, be sure to test your detector on a regular basis. Smoke alarms work by detecting the particles that float in the air when a fire occurs. The method used in smoke detection is either by optical detection, which is known as photoelectric, or by another process known as ionization. Some detectors also use a combination of both technologies.

The vast majority of the detectors installed in homes in the United States today use ionization technology. This detector is cheaper to produce than detectors that use photoelectric technology. Industry representatives for fire protection and prevention are hesitant to exclusively declare that one type of detector is better than the other, mainly because each one operates better under certain conditions. A flaming fire is detected slightly faster by an ionization sensor, where as a photoelectric detector responds quicker to a fire that is smoldering. Four states, namely Massachusetts, Vermont, Maine and Iowa have passed laws requiring homes to have photoelectric detectors.

In new homes, building codes often require that smoke detectors are hardwired into the home's electrical system. Wireless smoke detectors also can be linked to home security systems, along with other detection systems, such as those that measure a rapid rise in heat that may indicate fire.

In conjunction with having smoke alarms, you may also want to install a carbon monoxide detector. This is important if you have a gas-operated fireplace, stove, clothes dryer or furnace, and also if you use a portable heater, do indoor grilling or have an attached garage.

Fire Extinguishers

Fire extinguishers are classified into three categories or a combination of these.

Class "A" (common combustibles)

Class "B" (flammable liquids)

Class "C" (electrical fires)

In many home improvement stores you will find extinguishers that are classified to fight all three types of fire. Fire extinguishers come in various sizes and weights. The weight listing on the extinguisher refers to chemicals inside. According to the National Fire Protection Association (www.nfpa.org), you should have at least one fire extinguisher per floor of your home.

When using a fire extinguisher remember the PASS system – pull the pin, aim at the base of the fire, squeeze the handle and sweep from side to side. Realize that even a large extinguisher will last only around 20 seconds before being emptied.

If your smoke detector goes off, get out of the house as soon as possible, closing the doors behind you, and make sure all family members meet at a predetermined location safely away from the home before calling 911. Also, every year, have a designated time on your calendar that you change the battery on all smoke detectors.

As a homeowner, you need to make sure you are fully insured for any and all losses, including fire. This means having insurance that covers the full replacement value of your home. The reason for this is simple. You might think that, in the event of a fire, firefighters will go rushing in to save your home and all your valuables. Unfortunately, this simply is not reality-based.

Fighting the modern fires of today is based on both offensive attacks and defensive positions. There are three basic priorities firefighters have upon arriving on scene. The first of these is lifesaving, making sure all potential occupants are out of the building with no one left inside. Second, firefighters seek to stabilize, control and ultimately extinguish the fire. Finally, the last concern is the conservation of the property itself, seeking to reduce any damage caused by the fire.

Small fires can spread to out-of-control fires quickly. Fire extinguishers are needed not just in the kitchen, but in your bedroom as well.

Ask yourself the following questions: Do you have smoke detectors? Do you need to install a carbon monoxide detector? Do you have gas appliances, such as gas logs or a gas stove? If so, are they in proper working order? If you have a wood-burning stove or fireplace, when was the last time you had the stovepipe or chimney cleaned?

CHAPTER FOURTEEN

Other Ways to Ensure Home Safety

Home Inventory

If you had a home fire or some other disaster and little remained, could you give an account of your home's contents? A good exercise is to close your eyes and say aloud everything that is in the room you are in now while someone records your words on a sheet of paper. Once you can't remember any more details, stop and record all the items you missed. When you do this simple yet effective exercise, you will be convinced that the best way to protect yourself in the event of a disaster is to have a full home inventory.

I realize this can seem like an overwhelming and depressing task, and most of us avoid doing this, but we do so at our own peril. To overcome this hesitation, I have an exercise I would like you to complete. First, count the number of rooms in your home or apartment, including bathrooms and any garage or outbuilding you might have. Next, look at your calendar and place on your "to do" list a time where you can sit down and take a physical inventory of all the items in at least one room each day for the next two weeks. You will need to purchase an inexpensive spiral notebook and use a digital camera to take pictures of each item.

At the top of the page list the room. Next take a picture or walk around your home – room by room with a video recorder. If you are video recording, feel free to talk as you record. In your notebook, name each item, write a brief description of the item and include any serial number or model number, record the date of purchase and the amount you paid for it. If possible, you need to have the original receipt or a copy. Note that the ink on some cash register receipts will fade over time, so copies can be important. If you have a lot of expensive electronics, retain the user's manual to help verify ownership. If you charged your purchase on a credit card, retain a copy of the statement showing what you paid for the item.

In the event of a fire, break-in or other covered event, your insurance company will require you to file a claim listing what was lost or damaged. You need to contact your insurance agent, letting them know you are in the process of creating your home inventory, and ask them exactly what they would need to have in the event you needed to file a claim.

This would be an excellent time to identify what your limits are on your coverage. In the event your home was destroyed, does your insurance policy cover the full replacement value or does it only cover a set amount? With your newly created inventory you can determine the approximate value of the contents inside your home.

Does this match the stated insurance coverage amount?

Specifically ask what is NOT covered as well as what are the limits of coverage for items like silverware, guns, furs, artwork or other collectibles like coins.

An excellent and extensive home inventory documentation system called HomeManage Home Inventory Software has been developed by Liberty Street Software at http://www.libertystreet.com/. The great thing about this software package is it allows you to set up an electronic folder for each room in your house, list each item with descriptions and store multiple pictures, the purchase price and current market value.

The drawback of any computer software is the security of having this information on a computer that could be stolen or hacked into, if a fire occurs; unless a hard copy is printed and kept in a fireproof container this information could be lost.

Storage Unit Security

"The self-storage industry has been one of the fastest-growing sectors of the United States commercial real estate industry over the period of the last 35 years. There are now approximately 49,940 'primary' self-storage facilities in the United States as of year-end 2011; another 4,000 are 'secondary' facilities (primary means that self-storage is the primary source of business revenue – US Census Bureau). There are approximately 58,500 self-storage facilities worldwide as of Q4 – 2011; there are more than 3,000 in Canada and more than 1,000 in Australia. Total self-storage rentable space in the US is now 2.3 billion square feet (as of Q4-2011) [approximately 210 million square meters]. That figure represents more than 78 square miles of rentable self-storage space, under roof – or an area well more than 3 times the size of Manhattan Island (NY)."[59]

We are definitely a nation of stuff, and storage of our stuff has become epidemic.

The question you could ask yourself is do you REALLY need what you are storing? Is it worth what you will have to pay annually to store it? If you answered YES, then as you hunt for the right place to store your stuff you need to keep in mind the following concerns in regards to customer service, security, access and finally pricing.

Does the site where you are looking have an on-site manager or is it unattended? It is generally better to have someone close by that can be reached by phone during normal business hours, versus calls being only forwarded to a call center and then having to wait for a return phone call.

What is the age of the facility? Does the roof look to be in good shape, and have there been any flooding issues? What is the policy for food storage? Are there dumpsters on site to throw away trash? Does your unit have individual lighting or an electric plug that you can use? Pest control is a big concern! One rodent-infested unit can quickly spread to all the other units.

For security, is the facility surrounded by a fence and access-controlled with a key system or card access? Does the facility have security cameras, and do storage units have individual alarms or is this an option? Ride and look at the facility both during the day and at night. Is there proper lighting? Can your individual storage unit be accessed by climbing over a wall or by easily removing a side panel from the adjoining unit?

Before renting, it would be good to ask your local law enforcement if there has been any criminal activity in the area and if there have been any reported losses at the storage facility itself.

What are the hours of the facility, and are there any restrictions on how or when you are able to access your unit? Finally what does this cost? Is your rate locked in or does it change over time? Are there any administrative fees or deposits required? If the facility offers insurance, what does this specifically cover and not cover? Does your own homeowner's insurance cover your property stored away from your residence?

Protecting Your Home from Flooding

Most people by now are aware that your regular homeowner's policy does not protect you from rising water caused by a flood. For that you need to purchase a separate flood insurance policy. Also, in some areas of the country, due to the high water table, having water in your basement creates real problems and sump pumps are needed to keep everything dry.

The Cut-Off Quiz

Do you know how to cut off your gas, water or electricity? Do you know where the outside services are for your phone or cable? Do you have a control panel for an irrigation system or outdoor low-voltage lighting?

If you can answer the above questions, great! Make sure not only you, but others in your household, know the answers as well. You might want to keep the 4-in-1 Emergency Tool™ made by On Duty Inc. close by in the event you need it. http://www.onduty1.com/

Call Before You Dig!

As warmer weather approaches, many people like to get outside and plant flowers and bushes or work on other home projects. However, what started as a fun project can end up being a total aggravation that could cause serious personal injury for you, and potentially cause problems for everyone on your street if you happen to hit a utility line. At the very least, you could cut a phone line or disrupt your cable TV or burst a water pipe. To prevent you from possible injury or making an embarrassing mistake, you should first call 811, which is a federally mandated national "Call Before You Dig" number, before starting any major outdoor digging projects. Within a few days, a free utility locator service will stop by and mark the areas of concern so you know where you can safely dig.

Apartment or Condo Living

Before signing any lease, you need to find out what,

if any, issues have taken place at this location. Call and talk with the local law enforcement to determine what, if any, calls about criminal activity have come from that particular location. Next, fully survey the area where you plan on renting. Look at the location both during the day and night. Are parking areas well lit? If the complex has a garage how is it access protected – with a code or card system? Does the apartment complex or condo have security present? Does the complex have cameras, and if so is the video recorded and saved? How are doors secured? Can anyone walk into your building? Do stairways have adequate lighting and allow entrance only from the inside through one way doors? You need to also discuss how master keys are secured – if management will have access to your apartment or condo and when they will be used. If doorplates or mailboxes must have a name displayed do NOT make it gender specific. Instead, simply put an initial for your first name and then list your last name. Example: J. Jones.

Elevator Safety

When you use an elevator make sure when the door opens can you see entirely inside. Never ride in an elevator alone with a stranger. If you are in an elevator, let everyone else press their floor before you press yours, and position yourself closest to the control panel next to any alarm button, but with your back to the wall.

CHAPTER FIFTEEN

Automobile Safety

What Should You Carry?

You should always carry your driver's license with you. Also, while it might not be practical, you may want to consider carrying with you your car registration as well as insurance information. The reason behind this logic of having it on your person rather than in the car is simple. If someone breaks into a car, the first thing they are going to do is look above the sun visor and in the glove box for anything of value. Second, as mentioned earlier, if you have a garage door opener or a spare set of keys, this too can be an added bonus to a thief. Whatever you keep in your car you should keep it hidden and, if need be, locked in your glove box rather than out on your dash.

It is a good idea to have a writing pad as well as a pen or pencil. You may also want to consider having an emergency escape tool that allows you to cut your seatbelt as well as break out a side window. You need to make a habit of looking to see that you have a full tank of gas. Several additional items that most people should carry include a GPS that is up-to-date with the latest maps, a paper map of the area, a flashlight that works as well as a cell phone and a roll of duct tape. You should also think about carrying in your vehicle at all times an extra set of clothes, including socks and underwear, a small emergency medical kit, a roll of toilet paper and bottle of water.

Most people at one point in time will experience a tire failure on their vehicle. With this being a reality, you should know not only where a spare tire is located, but also how to change a tire. Most states require that if a car is sold it must have a functional spare tire, a jack and device to remove the lug nuts. Unfortunately, these tires are rarely full-sized, but smaller versions that should only be used on a temporary basis. You need to look to see what you have in your vehicle now before you need it and consider going to an auto parts store and purchasing a full size lug nut wrench that would allow you greater torque in removing the lug nuts off your wheels. You might also want to purchase and have in your vehicle a small foam mat used by gardeners so that kneeling on the pavement or grass won't be so uncomfortable. The foam mat can also be used to prevent the extra tools from rattling in your trunk.

One solution in helping prevent flat tires is a product that has been around for over forty-five years and was even used by NASA in the 1970's to protect the tires for the moon rover. This product is called Ultraseal and can be found online at http://www.ultraseal.com/. This product was manufactured to help extend the life of your tires by helping prevent total blowouts as well as stop slow leaks. This product works by using a formula to calculate the needs of your specific tire. Then the product is pumped into your fully inflated tire and then, by the use of centrifugal force, the product coats the interior of the tire. This automatically leaves a puncture resistant sealant that produces amazing results. I watched a video online of a car driving over a board with over a dozen nails puncturing a tire and yet it still remained fully inflated!

Another concept not widely discussed is the use of run flat tires. The ridge sidewall of these tires holds the weight of the vehicle, which allows someone to drive an extra fifty miles or so before having to stop. In doing research you will quickly find a number of reports stating both the pros and cons of installing these types of tires on your vehicle. Obviously you know your situation best. Whatever the case, it is good to know that these options now exist.

Driver's License & Registration Privacy

If you are concerned about privacy issues and you can go to the trouble of having an unlisted phone number, then you may also want to consider checking with the local office in your area that issues your state's driver's licenses. Specifically, you should ask about the legality of having, as your printed address, a post office box for both your driver's license and vehicle registration. Some states insist that a street address is required.

Are You Being Followed?

If you think you are being followed, the first thing you need to do is not panic! Second, make sure your doors are locked and windows secured. To know for certain if someone is actually following you, you should take these evasive actions: Turn left at the next corner then make another left and finally a right turn. If it is easier to turn right then do so twice then turn back left. By doing one of the above, if the vehicle is still behind you then you should NOT go to your planned destination, but instead drive to the nearest police or fire station or area with a large crowd to seek safety. If you have a cell phone you can dial 911 and tell the person who answers that you feel your life is in danger and tell them the street address where you are located and ask where you should go next.

Carjacking

The term "carjacking" did not exist until the 1990's; until then a car was simply stolen or hijacked. Carjacking is a traumatic crime that occurs when the perpetrator attempts to steal your vehicle, many times with you inside. These brazen, mostly male criminals display a weapon and use the threat of force to convince you to exit the vehicle.

In the United States there are approximately 38,000 carjackings annually. Of these, 45 percent attempts are successful at gaining access to the vehicle. Also it should be noted that 63 percent of the time carjacking happens when the victim is five miles or less from their home.

If you feel your life is in danger, comply with the carjacker's request and, when you exit, get away as quickly as possible.

Situations like this often occur when the car is stopped either at a stoplight or stop sign where your car is surrounded by a curb, making escape more difficult. Make sure that you *keep doors locked and windows closed at all times.* Another type of carjacking occurs when the perpetrator bumps into your car and waits for you to exit to assess the damage. Carjacking may also happen in areas like a parking garage, a shopping mall or grocery store, or by someone following you home from the mall or an ATM.

Lastly, a carjacker might pretend to be a law enforcement officer stopping your vehicle or handing you a ticket, or pretend to be a valet that will park your car for you. As with any dangerous situation, try to remain calm as possible, get a good description of the perpetrator, and contact law enforcement once you reach safety.

Combat Parking

Combat parking is a military term used to identify the method of parking a vehicle in such a way that you can escape quickly when necessary. This ready and alert mindset is an appropriate one that can easily be adapted to civilian life as you go about your everyday routine of driving to grocery stores and shopping malls. When you park, keep in mind the possible need for a quick drive-off, and don't box yourself in or require that you have to back up in order to leave. Another point to consider is when your vehicle is at a stop sign or stoplight; make sure to leave enough space between you and the vehicle in front of you. The easiest way to determine the right amount of space is to make sure that you see the vehicle's back tires.

Car Security Devices

If necessary, you may feel the need to add a Stolen Vehicle Recovery System (SVRS) to your vehicle. A well-known version most people have heard of is LoJack® at http://www.lojack.com/, which boasts a 90 percent recovery rate! You also might want to add a hidden kill switch that prevents your car from starting, or you might have an ignition cut off switch or a fuel switch wired in. All can be deterrents for those who wish to steal your car.

Valet Parking and Car Washes

When you go to a restaurant or mall that offers valet parking, make sure you only leave your ignition key with the attendant. The same can be said if you go to a car wash where an attendant vacuums and washes your car. Make sure you do not leave a checkbook or deposit receipt or any other information that includes your name and address and might pose a security risk. This includes junk mail. Remember to remove your registration and insurance card if you keep this in your car, and take them with you, as well as your garage door opener or any extra keys you may keep in the vehicle.

The reason: A valet attendant could easily write down your name and address and steal your garage door opener and then use it to break in later!

Unattended Trailer or Boat

If you tow an RV trailer or boat, you need to purchase an unattended coupler lock system like the one offered by Trimax™ at www.trimaxlocks.com and/ or their Trimax™ Trailer Wheel Locking system.

Don't leave keys in the ignition of your boat or have it idling at the dock as you go inside the store to pick up some supplies or pay for gas. Furthermore, you need to inventory all your equipment, including any electronics and other items you carry in both your boat and RV, and keep this list in a safe location and not with the boat or RV.

It is always a good idea to mark personal items, a permanent marker, engraving device or a UV pen, with your name and a driver's license number. All this can greatly enhance any chance of recovery if your boat or RV is stolen. If you own a boat make sure you have a record of the vessel hull identification number (HIN).

CHAPTER SIXTEEN

Travel Safety

Travel Pride

Getting ready to go on vacation can be exciting, and most of us look forward to getting away from our routine; however, in this excitement we tend to be careless.

Understandably, it is normal when we are on vacation and away from our everyday life we let our guard down. We all tend to pay less attention to what is going on around us. Unfortunately, in this day and time this can be very dangerous. In an idealistic world we would like to think that everyone is there to help us and there are no thieves around the corner. But this is simply not true. Our thought process concerning vacation should be a lot more than just not forgetting the sunscreen.

How well have we investigated the destination where we are going? The truth is most of us would like to totally believe everything we read or the pictures we see on the hotel websites. However, we all have had instances where upon arrival we were extremely disappointed because things were not as they were described.

Fortunately, in our modern world of instant communication you will find websites like www.tripadvisor.com or www.yelp.com that allow you to read reviews on not only hotels and restaurants, but on the things to do at your destination. Typically these reviews do not specifically point out any security dangers, so for this information you need to investigate deeper.

If you are traveling in the United States, one of the quickest and best ways to find out how safe an area is for you to travel is to simply contact the local city or county law enforcement agency by phone and talk to a crime prevention officer. These individuals are going to give you a better picture of what is truly happening in the area than someone from the local chamber or convention and visitors' bureau. Simply tell the officer the dates when you are planning on traveling to the area and that you would like to know if the hotel where you are staying is safe. Also ask if there have been any recent concerns in the area. Specifically, what types of crime have been occurring at your destination? Are cars being broken into in certain parking lots? Are there certain areas of high-gang activity?

The next thing you need to do to pre-plan for your trip is to go online for at least the next week before you travel and read the local newspaper and specifically pay attention to any mention of criminal activity.

Traveling Overseas

If you plan on traveling overseas then you may want to sign up for the free Smart Traveler Enrollment

Program (STEP) at https://step.state.gov/step/. By doing so you will automatically get Travel Warning and Travel Alerts and the latest up-to-date information on the conditions for the country you plan on traveling to.

Also you should visit www.travel.state.gov as well as www.worldaware.org to check the area where you are traveling. Also review the information from the State Department's Office of American Citizen Services and Crisis Management that is found online at http://travel.state.gov/law/citizenship/citizenship_775.html.

"The State Department's Office of American Citizen Services and Crisis Management (ACS) is here to assist you and your family whenever and wherever we can. We work with our overseas embassies and consulates to provide emergency services to Americans abroad. We can help send money overseas to assist U.S. citizens, repatriate the remains of loved ones who have died, assist victims of crime, and help U.S. citizens who are detained in foreign prisons. ACS also administers a repatriation loan program to bring home destitute Americans. We operate a 24-hour Duty Officer Program."[60]

If you plan on traveling overseas and are a United States citizen, then you need to have in your cell phone the following phone numbers for the Overseas Citizen Services: To reach the office from within the United States you can call toll free at 888-407-4747. If you are calling outside the United States you need to call 202-501-4444.

Before leaving the country make sure to check with your cell phone carrier to see if your phone will operate overseas. If it will not, you need to consider renting a phone for your journey with an international number.

Preparing To Leave

First, we don't think about who might be watching us load our luggage in the car, or about the negative consequences of broadcasting our vacation to others. Likewise, loading the car at night, hoping to get an early start the next morning, might not be a good idea after all. Nothing could ruin a vacation more than to discover your luggage was stolen.

Remember, before you leave your home you need to walk around and make sure ALL your windows and doors are locked and secure. This includes your garage doors and any out buildings. If you have a remote control door on your garage, make sure it is unplugged or the switch is turned off at your breaker panel. Make sure any important valuables, as well as items like jewelry and firearms, are stored in a locked and secure safe or closet.

The main objective you should seek to achieve is making your house look normal and lived in, but secure. Keep your air conditioner or heating unit on. The best possible scenario would be to have an actual house sitter stay in your home while you are away or come and go to check on your home. If this is not a reasonable option, or you are going to be gone for a short period of time, then make sure you leave the blinds in a normal position and turn your phone ringer as low as possible. Several lights should be on timers and set, if possible, to flip on and off at random. If you use a yard irrigation system keep this on as you normally would.

Make sure to have someone pick up any newspapers as well as your mail and check for any packages that might arrive unexpectedly. A common ruse some burglars use to see if people are home is to stick a pizza flyer in the door. If the flyer isn't retrieved after a few days, the burglar knows no one is home.

If you have to, you can place a hold on your mail between three and thirty days, and when you return pick your mail up at the Post Office. To do this you need to make your request online at https://holdmail.usps.com/holdmail/. You can also go to the post office branch that services your address and make your request known by filling out a form they provide you. If you find that you are going to be gone longer than thirty days, you can use the US Post Office Premium Forwarding Service®. You have to pay a fee to enroll and then pay a weekly fee for your mail to be boxed and forwarded to you. To learn more go to the following website address: https://www.usps.com/manage/forward-mail.htm.

The drawback to canceling a newspaper delivery or placing a hold on your mail is that, by doing so, you have unknowingly told six or more people your vacation plans. It always is better to have a neighbor or trusted friend or family member retrieve both your newspaper and mail daily.

Don't forget about your trash or recycling pick up. Have a neighbor roll back any cans from the street and put them in the normal spot. If you are planning to be gone for several weeks, ask a neighbor to place some of their trash in your can and put it in front of your home during the regular pickup time to make it appear someone is still at home.

If you are a two-car family, and plan to be gone a long time, have a next-door neighbor move your car to a different location in your driveway every few days. If you only have one car, and have taken this on your trip, then ask them to park one of their cars in your driveway.

Note that today, with social media sites like Facebook™, people are giving out more information to all types of people, many of whom are really not the "friends" we think they might be. Announcing that you are going on a lavish two-week vacation tells everyone that your house will be vacant for two weeks and that now is a perfect time to break in and steal all your valuables. It is best to avoid talking at the barbershop or beauty salon or bragging to your coworkers about your upcoming vacation.

In World War II, the War Advertising Council created a phrase for a poster that read, "Loose lips sink ships." We would be wise to heed this warning as it applies to our personal and home security. Think about this phrase before you post online that real-time beautiful sunset photo. Note, too, that unless you disable certain features on sites like Facebook™, the location of your post will automatically be identified as well.

Sidebar: We all need to be reminded that paradise is where you make it! You always take yourself with you, so if you are not totally happy at home then you are not going to be one hundred percent satisfied just because you go on vacation.

Luggage

With the advent of the Transportation Security Administration, otherwise known as TSA, many people now leave their luggage unlocked; however, this is not necessary. You can still lock your luggage, and it is advisable to do so. "TSA screens every passenger's baggage before it is placed on an airplane. While our technology allows us to electronically screen bags, there are times when we need to physically inspect a piece of luggage. TSA has worked with several companies to develop locks that can be opened by security officers using universal "master" keys so that the locks may not have to be cut. These locks are available at airports and travel stores nationwide. The packaging on the locks indicates whether they can be opened by TSA."[61]

Several additional tips concern tagging your bag for identification: First, consider placing a brightly colored or unique ribbon or cloth around the handle of your luggage to help avoid someone taking your luggage by mistake. Second, place both on the outside and inside of your luggage identification that has your name, a business address or a post office box, but NEVER your home address. Also include on the tag your cell phone number. Note that expensive designer luggage draws unwanted attention and should be avoided, especially when flying and traveling overseas.

The reason for not using your home address is simple. An airport worker or anyone handling your luggage could notify others that you have taken a trip, and this home address will likely be vacant and open for burglary. It should go without saying, but watch your baggage at all times and keep a record of what is in your luggage. Don't accept gifts from strangers, any gift no matter how small! Keeping watch on your luggage also means following the bellman, not just assuming he or she will bring the luggage to you.

When possible, fly nonstop to your destination; this tends to decrease the chance of lost luggage. Place inside your luggage a sealed envelope that has a printout of your travel schedule, including the name and phone number of all the hotel destinations on your schedule, as well as a photo copy of your driver's license and/or passport. The hotel phone numbers should also be plugged into your cell phone in advance of you leaving. Make sure a copy of all this information is left with a friend or family member and you may want to include with this information a certified copy of your birth certificate and a duplicate driver's license, if you have one.

If you have prescription glasses, contacts, vitamins, denture products, baby products or other certain medications, it is best to have these in a carry on with you versus packing them in your suitcase. Make sure that any medications you bring are kept in the original pill container with your name on it – especially prescription drugs that are narcotic in nature.

Travel Insurance

Often vacations can be expensive adventures, but unexpected things can happen where your plans have to be delayed or canceled due to a medical emergency. To help protect you from these unforeseen events, you can buy an insurance product called trip insurance. There are lots of different companies online that offer this type of coverage, so it would be wise for you to explore all the different options to see which one is right for you. Most of these companies offer insurance in the event you have to cancel your trip or it is interrupted or delayed.

Most of the time we are not thinking about the possibility of a medical emergency, but accidents and sickness can happen. A vacation can quickly turn into a nightmare if you find that your current health insurance does not cover certain medical expenses away from home. Since this is a real risk, it is worth the time and energy to investigate the cost of purchasing insurance that covers any medical expense that might occur while on vacation. Make sure to check to see if this insurance also covers any pre-existing medical condition that might force you to cancel or delay your trip.

Some insurance covers the possibility of a missed airline connection because of weather or an airline delay, as well as delays in receiving your luggage. Certain products cover events like cruise line or tour operators defaulting on their promise to provide you with a service.

As with all insurance products, there are certain limitations and exclusions, and you have to read all the fine print before agreeing to any contract and paying the stated fee. Finally, in order to secure trip insurance, the company providing the insurance will likely want to know the state where you live and the country you plan on traveling to. They will also want to know your date of birth to determine your age and the amount of time you will be away.

Rental Car Security and Insurance

You are at the rental car counter and you are asked if you want to opt in for their collision damage waiver, which covers any damage while you have the car, and this includes theft of the car. You see the extra fee and you wonder if you should or shouldn't accept this option.

Your answer depends on several questions you need to have answered before you decide to rent. First, ask your insurance agent if you are already covered under your personal car insurance. If you are charging your car rental using a credit card, some credit card companies provide this coverage as a benefit if you charge the rental on their card. You need to call in advance and understand their policy. In most cases, but not all, this extra "insurance" is NOT needed.

An important tip to consider when renting a vehicle is to pick one that has automatic door locks and air conditioning so you can stay secure in the vehicle and do not have to have your windows rolled down.

Your Money or Your Life!

Flashing a wad of cash has never been safe, but today's world is becoming more dangerous, where anyone and everyone can become a target. The less you stand out, the better. When you are on vacation, or even at home shopping, you should consider not wearing expensive jewelry, specifically watches or rings. Likewise, it is always better to go with someone and to try to park as close to the door as possible.

Pay special attention when you are riding public transportation and walking in parking lots or places that are remote. Pulling out large amounts of cash attracts unwanted attention and it is never advised. You should also be extra careful when you are at an ATM, and again it is better to have two people present – with one making the transaction while the other looks out for any activity in the area. Try to avoid making ATM transactions at night and in poorly lit or desolate places.

Pick Pocketing

Pick pocketing is quite common and normally occurs by someone bumping into you to distract you with another reaching and stealing a wallet from an open purse or off your person. These thieves typically work in groups, and if a wallet or money is taken it is quickly passed off to someone else going in the opposite direction.

In the United States, the "art" or crime of pick pocketing is a relatively rare occurrence. However, overseas, in countries like France, you will see an entirely different picture. A September 19, 2013, *New York Times* article reported that The Louvre Museum, which attracts as many as 25,000 to 30,000 visitors daily and is the world's most visited museum, temporarily closed after two hundred security and surveillance agents went on strike due to the growing violence of those who were pick pocketing the guards themselves, as well as the tourists.

As a traveler, it is important to learn how to protect yourself against these threats. Wrap several rubber bands around any money or credit cards. This causes friction, making it more difficult to remove unnoticed. Try to limit the amount of money and credit cards you carry and avoid sitting or standing near doors, especially on a subway. Beware of the friendly stranger asking you for directions or trying to sell you trinkets or asking you to sign a petition. Another common technique is for one person to spill ice cream or throw water on you and then others rush in to pretend to offer help.

It is important to remember that outside pockets and or purses are the "target." Instead of placing items in a pants or shirt pocket or allowing them to dangle by your side, you STRONGLY need to consider other alternatives. Various companies sell tee shirts that have pouches or zippered pockets under the arms or at chest height. There are also pouches that snap to a women's bra.

At one time the term "money belt" used to describe a literal zipper pouch that was made into a belt you would wear around your waist. Now this term incorporates a whole host of other devices that include men's or women's underwear that have zipper pouches built in. You can find zipper pouches that loop over a belt and tuck inside your pants, or a separate band altogether, that is secured around your waist that you wear under your regular clothing. People have also used elastic banded items with a pouch around their arm, as well as underneath pants on their leg. Regardless, you need to find something that works for you, and you should not wait until you go on a trip to try it out. Make a point to wear the device or devices a few days before you travel to make sure it is something you can live with. You don't want something to feel binding nor do you want something that easily slips off.

I would NOT recommend you use any device that hangs around your neck or buy a purse or other item like a camera strap that has a cut resistant strap. The reason is simple – if someone is willing to yank something off your neck, or use a knife to take something away from you by force, then it is not worth the risk of getting hurt to resist such an attack.

If you are traveling with a passport, make sure you carry copies in your suitcase or carry on. If your hotel room has a safe then use it, or if you have a way to secure important documents or valuables in a hotel safe you should do so. There are also a number of different diversion safes as well that may be used. These "safes" look either like articles of clothing or are items that look like ordinary toiletry items, like a can of shaving cream.

A few places to find items to help make your trip more secure:

http://solotravelerblog.com/solo-travel-safety-gear/

http://www.catch22products.co.uk/Securitymoney.htm

http://www.ricksteves.com/plan/tips/theft.htm

Looking Good

Being a tourist does not mean you have to advertise the fact. Try to blend in versus standing out in a crowd. Avoid wearing items like a "fanny pack," and limit the time you carry a camera or camera bag so that you don't scream "tourist."

Maps are good to carry discreetly, but don't stand around in the middle of the street looking lost. You need to move with a purpose versus wandering aimlessly. If you have to ask for directions, ask a family with small kids, not a lone stranger.

Jewelry should be worn at a minimum, and never dress in a provocative manner. When traveling, especially overseas, do not wear expensive designer clothes or carry designer accessories. Also avoid wearing tee shirts or other clothing advertising your nationality. Do not dress in anything that might give someone the impression you are part of any military group.

While all these tips might seem common sense when you travel or go on a vacation, each and every one of them is worth mentioning as a review.

It is helpful to have written down, as well as programmed in your cell phone, the local emergency numbers as well as the phone number of the place where you are staying. However, depending on where you are located, you need to realize that you may not have cell service. When you check in to your hotel, ask for a business card that has the hotel's address and phone number. These are great to be able to show a taxi driver.

If you travel by taxi, ask someone at the hotel to

call one for you and ask at the front desk if there are any safety concerns you need to be aware of in the area, such as pick pockets or other incidences.

If you are approached by a person asking for money, even a small child, ignore the request and tell them no.

CHAPTER SEVENTEEN
Hotel Safety

People rarely think about hotel security when checking into a hotel. However, consider asking front desk personal as well as any bellman if there are any areas near the hotel that you should avoid. Also, be alert to your surroundings and watch your belongings, taking special note of who else might be standing nearby. Women traveling alone should consider registering using a first initial and their last name, or register under both Mr. and Mrs. instead of identifying themselves as traveling alone.

Front desk personnel checking you in should never announce your name loudly, and especially not your room number. Ask the hotel front desk staff if a key is required to enter the exterior doors of the hotel at night and if they have any security officers on duty. If you feel the least bit uncomfortable, you should ask for assistance in taking your belongings to your room. One of the more vulnerable moments you have in a hotel is what is known as a push-in robbery, which occurs at the time where you are distracted with your luggage and pulling the key out to enter into the room.

Once in your room, lock the door and consider placing a cheap rubber door wedge under the door. You can also purchase a battery operated door wedge that triggers a loud alarm when activated. A low-tech way to make noise is to take your key ring and, if there is sufficient space, take one key and place it on the top doorframe and have the other keys of your ring dangle down. If someone tries to open the door the keys will fall, making a noise.

Note: When you leave your room for the day DO NOT put the sign on the door requesting housekeeping to clean your room. This sign is actually an invitation for a thief; in essence you are sending a message that your room is empty.

Choosing Your Room

Ground floor rooms are more often targeted for a break-in because it is easier and quicker to walk in and walk out. For this reason, consider booking a room on a second or higher floor. However, higher is not always better, keep reading to understand why!

Hotel Fire

If you travel around the world you should not stay above the fourth floor of a hotel, and if you are in the United States never above the eighth floor. The reason is simple, while you might have the best view, firefighters do not have the ability to fight fires above these levels.

If you do suspect a fire, call the front desk. Next feel the door for heat. If the door feels hot do not open it;

instead, place a wet towel at the threshold of the door and turn off the air conditioner.

If the door feels cool, first check to make sure you have your door key with you, then look on the back of the door and identify the direction to the nearest exit. Next place a wet hand towel over your face and mouth and walk quickly to the nearest exit or stairway. Do not use the elevators. If the smoke is too thick to see, then crawl to the nearest exit. If you have a flashlight with you, make sure you carry it with you as you exit.

Hotel Room Doors and Locks

We all have seen the hotels that use the hotel security door guard consisting of ball lock and latch locking systems. Locks that consist of a round metal ball on one end and a hasp latching system on the other are supposed to prevent a maid or someone that has a key from walking in if the door is locked. Well, this can easily be hacked by using a flexible piece of stiff plastic. When the door is opened, you slide the plastic piece against the U-shaped hasp and push it clear to open the door.

In 2012, at a security conference in Las Vegas, it was revealed that a specific electronic lock currently installed in four million hotel rooms was considered vulnerable to attack using a digital tool that is inserted into the lock to open the door. Furthermore, an article in Forbes Magazine stated that, while the company released a temporary fix for this problem, the only way to permanently fix the problem is to replace the circuit board in the lock. The company that made the lock is not covering that cost, but is expecting the hotel to cover the replacement cost.[62]

I'm sure all this will result in a long legal battle, but in the meantime these facts beg the question: Are people in hotel rooms really safe? Beyond the noted digital threat to opening your door, another vulnerability comes to us by way of the well-meaning ADA Accessibility Guidelines 4.13.9, which states the following concerning door hardware: "Handles, pulls, latches, locks, and other operating devices on accessible doors shall have a shape that is easy to grasp with one hand and does not require tight grasping, tight pinching, or twisting of the wrist to operate. Lever-operated mechanisms, push-type mechanisms, and U-shaped handles are acceptable designs. When sliding doors are fully open, operating hardware shall be exposed and usable from both sides. Hardware required for accessible door passage shall be mounted no higher than 48 in (1220 mm) above finished floor."

Locksmiths have developed a simple tool that you can buy online for a mere $60. For that, you receive a long metal rod that can be slid under a door and turned upwards to hook the handle to open the door from the inside. The only fix for this vulnerability at this point is to make sure that the bottom of the door has very little clearance to the floor. To make it harder to open the door, you can wedge a towel in the handle of the door itself.

Another method of entry involves removing the peephole and sliding in a device to pull the handle to open the door. If you are concerned that this might occur, place superglue around the peephole on the room side of the door and wipe away the excess glue. Once this dries it should make unscrewing the peephole much more difficult.

Bed Bugs

Depending on your age, you may have heard as a child, "Good night, sleep tight, don't let the bed bugs bite!" Unfortunately, it seems, while bed bugs were thought to be mostly eradicated in the 1940's, these insects have made a major resurgence within the last decade.

Adult bed bugs are small, wingless, nocturnal, oval-shaped insects that are red to brown in color and one-eighth to one-quarter inch in size. The egg of a bed bug is extremely small, white in color, and the size of several grains of salt. Their diet consists of blood from other warm-blooded animals, but they prefer humans and are drawn by the release of carbon dioxide and body heat. The adult insects are flat as a sheet of paper before they are fed, and they look like a small drop of blood after feeding. What makes these insects unique is that they can live as long as six months without food. Due to their tiny shape and size, they hide in cracks and crevices and attach themselves easily by traveling in suitcases and on clothing.

When a bed bug bites a person, the individual is unaware because the bug injects an anesthetic at the location of the bite as well as an anticoagulant that keeps the blood from clotting, allowing them to extract the blood. Within several days of being bitten, some people suffer a mild to moderate skin reaction. This presents itself as a red area that can be slightly swollen and itch, while other individuals show no symptoms at all.

In 2006, a free public online database was established at http://bedbugregistry.com/ This database allows users in the United States and Canada to submit a report identifying the source of any infestation. Since its inception, approximately 12,000 locations have been identified in 20,000 reports submitted.

The number one thing you can do to protect yourself against bed bugs when you travel is be observant. Prior to making any reservations, look online and read the travel reviews for the destination you plan on visiting. When you arrive at the place you plan on staying for the night, look to see how clean it looks, specifically look at the mattresses and box springs of the bed where you will be sleeping. If you see ANY signs of bugs, request another room or go somewhere else.

Since bedbugs are known to be professional hitchhikers, the luggage people carry has become a prime source for their ability to move from location to location easily and, unfortunately this includes back to the traveler's home. To thwart this unwanted guest, a company has developed a set of luggage called Thermal Strike, which is actually luggage that, when plugged in and turned on, heats itself up to 140 degrees Fahrenheit for 2.5 hours, killing any bedbugs that may be inside, see http://www.thermalstrike.com/ While this luggage is expensive at more than $300 per piece, it pales in comparison to the cost of having your entire home exterminated.

In-Room Safes – Are They Really Safe?

Most of the larger hotels in America have in room safes. Most of us appreciate the convenience of having what appears to be a good option to store valuables like extra jewelry, cash or your airline tickets while you are out. Some newer safes even have a place to plug in your laptop computer, letting it charge while it sits. However, to protect yourself it is important that you are aware of the fatal flaws with this "security feature."

First, the mere fact that hotels have in-room safes means they likely have someone in charge of general maintenance with an override key or electric pass code device to unlock the safe. Even more disturbing is the fact that some safes are preset at the factory to open automatically by simply pressing all zeroes, regardless of the previously punched combination. Still other safes have been known to open by banging on the top or bottom of the safe. So, how's that for security?

To compound matters, the innkeeper laws in most states greatly limit the hotel liability for items that may be replaced if stolen. To protect yourself, you need to first call your insurance agent and check to see what, if anything, your homeowner policy covers when you are away from home.

Some hotels have lock boxes at the front desk for guests to use that you may want to consider.

While not perfect, there is a device call Milockie®, http://www.milockie.com, that is made in the U.K. but can be purchased through Amazon.com. What this device does is, in effect, place a lock on a locked safe using a strap system that threads from inside the safe itself. If nothing else, using this device could alert you to someone tampering with the safe while you are away.

Hotel Trash Can

Another aspect of hotel security is really a carryover from the discussion earlier of being aware of what you are throwing way and the information it might contain. Think carefully about what you are throwing away in the trashcan in your hotel room. Could this information in some way be turned into cash? You need to take home to destroy all documents, including such things like receipts that contain your name or credit card information.

Hot Tub and Pool Dangers

The Center for Disease Control and Prevention, otherwise known as the CDC reports that between 8,000 to as many as 18,000 people annually are hospitalized in the United States for Legionella, more commonly known as Legionnaires' Disease, which is a type of pneumonia. The Legionella germ is microscopic and naturally found in water, especially hot water. The germ is commonly found in swimming pools and hot tubs. However, there are reported cases of the germ also being transmitted through air condition cooling towers, as well as other plumbing systems, and via decorative fountains and pools. Regardless, the point of infection occurs when an individual breathes in the vapor mist or steam from water.

For the average traveler, the threat of contracting this germ is rare, but there are several precautions you may want to take before using a public pool or hot tub. Does the water look clear or cloudy? One test is to toss a coin in to see if you can identify if it is facing up or down. Does the pool have a bad odor? While chlorine is a commonly used disinfectant, it can be toxic as well, so you need to make sure there is proper ventilation. If you have small children you may want to talk to your pediatrician about the safety of chlorine exposure and the importance of showering before and after you spend time in a pool or hot tub. Is there a slimy film on the side of the pool?

Since your health is at risk, it is up to you to ask the owner or operator how the pool or hot tub you plan to use are maintained!

The following are a set of questions from the CDC concerning hot tubs that you may want to ask the owner or operator:

- What was the most recent health inspection score for the hot tub?
- Are disinfectant and pH levels checked at least twice per day?
- Are disinfectant and pH levels checked more often when the hot tub is being used by a lot of people?
- Are the following maintenance activities performed regularly?
  (a) Removal of the slime or biofilm layer by scrubbing and cleaning?
  (b) Replacement of the hot tub water filter according to manufacturer's recommendations?
  (c) Replacement of hot tub water?

CHAPTER EIGHTEEN
Preparedness

The Basics

My hope for you as you have read this book is that you have found topics covered interesting, as well as discovered some hidden truths you may not have been aware of and this has motivated you to take action. As you are aware by now, the act of being prepared does not occur randomly nor is it something you can do just one time; it is an ongoing event. The bulk of the topics of this book have been tailored toward looking specifically at your privacy and security, both at home and abroad.

However, as we draw to a close in this final section, I will briefly cover a few of the basic survival related topics I think you need to be aware of, as well as expose you to various other facts in an effort to make sure that you are ready to face any situation that comes your way.

Early Warning System

Many communities have an early warning system administered by either a county or city governmental agency that typically contacts you via phone with an emergency message. Some areas also have warning sirens or horns. Many television stations offer a free severe weather alert service that notifies you via a text message. The Red Cross and other groups offer apps you can download to your smart phone to make you aware of threats that could occur, which include: hurricanes, tornados, earthquakes and flooding.

If you have school-aged children, then you need to know in advance the school system policy surrounding any evacuation that may take place. One important question to ask is where will the students be taken in the event of an emergency?

Pet care is also a concern that needs to be thought about well in advance of needing to evacuate. If your animal does not normally ride in your vehicle, then you need to have in place a container they can ride in that is secure. You also need to have an ample supply of pet food and litter, if needed, on hand now versus trying to secure this during bad weather or an emergency situation.

It has been mentioned before, but it is worth repeating, that you should think about carrying in your vehicle at all times an extra set of clothes, including socks and underwear, a small emergency medical kit, and several bottles of water. You might also want to keep an extra roll of toilet paper in your car. Second, you should have a copy of any important documents you might need in case of an emergency. These documents do not have to always be on your person, but it helps to have a copy in a secure location that is not your main residence. In addition, you may want to consider having these documents scanned and on a thumb drive. If there are any prescription drugs that you need then those, too, should be in one location and easily accessible in the event of an emergency.

Basic Survival

The list is simple: air, water, food, shelter and sanitation.

Every morning we wake up, and most of us first go to the bathroom. Flushing the toilet, taking a shower and washing our face are routine. Electricity, water, sewer and gas services are all part of living in the modern age. But what happens when the normal routine of life is interrupted?

Daily we take these services for granted, even though we know we shouldn't. Yet, few of us ever think about having a back-up plan detailing what we would do in case of an emergency or a prolonged outage due to a severe storm. At some point we might all be asking one another the question: Where were you when the lights went out? If this were the case, would you be one of the ones who survive, or would you be lost and looking for others to take care of you?

Experts will tell you that it is possible to survive 20-plus days without food, but only about three days without clean water to drink before you will die. It is imperative that you are prepared to be able to have fresh drinking water no matter where you live!

The question you start to ask yourself is at what point are you relying on others to supply these basic needs, and how much of these needs can you supply on your own and for how long?

Breathe Deep

We all take for granted that the air we breathe every second is not only going to be available, but clean and safe to breathe. Remember, when preparing any kit you keep at home, work or in your car for responding to a disaster, be sure you have a N95 respirator, i.e. a dust mask that fits snugly over your nose and mouth. This product, when worn properly, should filter 95 percent of airborne particles to help keep you safe.

Water – Take Immediate Action

Since it is a proven fact that you cannot live very long without water, if you take your survival seriously you need to think what you would do in the event of a water system failure.

You will likely hear people say you should have one gallon of water per person per day. This gallon of water is not only for consumption, but for cooking and hygiene as well. If you want to have a little fun and try an experiment, on your next trip to the grocery store buy three one-gallon jugs of regular water. Start on Friday and don't take a shower, and turn off the water valve going to your toilet. Over a weekend use just the one-gallon bottle of water a day to eat, and wash your hands and face, etc. Do this all day Friday, Saturday and Sunday. Don't turn the water back on until first thing Monday morning.

So, how did you do? Not as easy as you thought is it? So do you really think you could live or survive long with such a little amount of water?

Below you will find a few "Water Trivia Facts" offered by the U.S. EPA that should be eye opening!

- American residents use about 100 gallons of water per day.
- Americans use more water each day by flushing the toilet than they do by showering or any other activity.
- At 50 gallons per day, residential Europeans use about half of the water that residential Americans use.
- Residents of sub-Saharan Africa use only two to five gallons of water per day.
- The average faucet flows at a rate of two gallons per minute. You can save up to four gallons of water every morning by turning off the faucet while you brush your teeth.
- Taking a bath requires up to 70 gallons of water. A five-minute shower uses only ten to twenty-five gallons.
- A running toilet can waste up to 200 gallons of water per day.
- A gallon of water weighs 8.34 pounds.

Now that you know the facts, I do recommend that you have some storage containers that are specifically food-grade material – made for water storage – and have a supply on hand. However, keep in mind the above fact that just one gallon of water weighs 8.34 pounds!

Many people get carried away and buy huge barrels to fill, but quickly realize that it is not practical for them to move the barrel and that they have no way to pump the water out. Some people also opt to stock up cases of bottled water. While having this is better than having nothing, it is important to know that the plastic that these bottles are made from can be thin and can break down over time and leak out. Also, if you keep these in a garage that is not climate controlled, they may freeze and burst. Finally, over time water can absorb odor, causing it to taste bad. You need to be aware of this and plan accordingly, rotating your water supply at least once a year.

Most people in the United States obtain their water from either a municipal water system or from their own well system. The following are products you should consider having on hand in order to create a supplemental supply in the event your main source of water fails.

Hydration Technology Innovations HTI™ offers a wide range of personal desalination and personal water filtration products. HydroPack™ is a disposable, one-time use pouch that is self-hydrating. To learn more, visit the following website: http://www.htiwater.com

Katadyn Products Inc., http://www.katadyn.com/usen/ , has developed an amazing solid steel pump that has a filter made from silver with a filtration life of an amazing 13,000 gallons of water before the filter needs to be replaced.

If you have advanced warning, like knowing a hurricane will likely hit your area, then you should consider purchasing a product called a WaterBOB® that can be found online at http://www.waterbob.com. This fold out, food grade plastic liner fits in your tub and allows you to store approximately one hundred gallons of fresh drinking water in your tub.

Food

The modern society in which we live is built around a just-in-time design. This means that the grocery store you visit to get your food is constantly being stocked with supplies on a weekly basis or less for most items. A failure in the supply chain can mean outages of goods that would be noticeable in just a few days, especially if a crisis situation arose and there was a panicked buying binge by the general public. Trust me when I say that you do not want to be in a grocery store when a crisis occurs being the one holding the last can of green beans!

A simple way to prepare is to buy a few extra cans of food each time you go shopping and label the food with the date you purchased it. Remember to buy only the foods you normally eat. If you feel compelled to purchase freeze dried or dehydrated food that is good for long-term food storage, do so only after test sampling the products you are buying to make sure they are actually something you would eat.

Since you have labeled the food as you purchased it, you should be able to rotate your stock and keep the food fresh so nothing is wasted. Remember, if you are considering storing food, keep it in a cool dry location, preferably inside. Also, if you are storing packaged food or items like sugar and flour, then it is advisable to place these in sealable plastic bags and then in sealable containers as an extra layer of protection.

The United States government has created a website: http://www.ready.gov/. If you go to this site you will find they have several recommendations when you consider creating an emergency food supply. It is recommended that you store at least a three-day supply. You need to make sure the foods you have on hand are foods that your family can eat and will eat. Also keep in mind as you make your preparations any dietary restrictions you or your family members may have. It is also suggested that you not eat food high in salt that will make you want to consume more water, and it is suggested that you eat whole grains and canned food that has a high liquid content. Think of living in an environment with no availability of power and refrigeration. You also need to take into consideration the utensils and other paper products that you will need for cooking and eating.

Waste Not, Want Not

Research from August 2012 by the Natural Resources Defense Council (NRDC) confirmed an amazing and startling statistic, "Getting food from the farm to our fork eats up 10 percent of the total U.S. energy budget, uses 50 percent of U.S. land, and swallows 80 percent of all freshwater consumed in the United States. Yet, 40 percent of food in the United States today goes uneaten. This not only means that Americans are throwing out the equivalent of $165 billion each year, but also that the uneaten food ends up rotting in landfills as the single largest component of U.S. municipal solid waste, where it accounts for a large portion of U.S. methane emissions. Reducing food losses by just 15 percent would be enough food to feed more than 25 million Americans every year at a time when one in six Americans lack a secure supply of food to their tables."[63]

So you might be wondering, what is the primary cause for this food loss? To put it in simple terms, "we," meaning the general public, are grossly misinformed! As much as 90 percent of Americans throw away edible food because they look at the "use by," "sell by" or "best before" label and think that if the product is beyond that specific date it must be "bad" and unusable, which is not entirely accurate. This date is supposed to coincide with the peak freshness of the product, not the date of spoilage. This date is also touted to be a tool to help retailer merchants manage their inventory better, so the storyline goes. However, if you are more pessimistic in your assumptions, having this date could very well be a way to encourage consumers to buy more products. So now that you know the truth, you won't be so fast tossing out all that GOOD food!

Shelter

If you have gotten to this point in the book, it is my hope that you feel pretty comfortable in your ability to protect yourself and your property. Having a place to lay your head at night and rest comfortably is important, not only for your personal safety, but your mental health as well.

More than likely, at some point in your lifetime, you will be faced with having to live through some sort of natural disaster. This disruption from your normal life may last a day or a few days or perhaps even longer.

A lot of hype has been given to the topic of "bugging out." The logic goes something like this. The threat that you face is so large and looming; there is a supposed army of roving marauders who plan on breaking into your home to kill you so they can steal all your valuables and food. So in order to prevent this from happening, "the experts" tell you that the solution is to leave behind your current safe haven and venture to a new and safer location. The objective is to hide or get further away from the masses of people and magically start a new life for yourself. For me at least, I cannot see the logic behind this drastic action. Few people are willing to leave all the possessions they cannot carry, stop working and, therefore, have no income to survive, as well as abandon extended family and friends to live life as a refugee. How is this safer?

Regardless, if you look specifically at the topic of having adequate shelter, there is something more realistic that you do need to think about – your answers to several simple questions.

First, I would ask you to make the assumption that NO utilities are operational and if you travel you can only do so by foot. This means no electricity, no water, no sewer or gas, and no vehicle, not even a bicycle! So, how long can you survive at home?

This introspective look requires you to establish

your own level of comfort, but it also begs the question of not just having stuff, but being able to know how to use it. A good analogy I read recently stated it this way: Having a surfboard does not make you a surfer!

Just having boxes of supplies does not ensure your complete survival. You need to have a plan and know what to do next. Also, while you are thinking about what you are going to do for yourself and your family, again think about any furry four-legged friends you may have and what their needs are as well.

Sanitation

Sanitation is more than just personal hygiene to make sure you smell good; it is a matter of protecting you against sickness and disease. Again, if you use the above scenario you need to ask yourself what is your plan for disposal of waste as well as bathing?

It is important that in ALL situations you encounter that you are never forced to only rely on ONE method or device for your personal safety and security. ALWAYS strive to have multiple options to choose from.

Medical Needs

If you are on certain medicines that your body needs in order to survive, you need to strongly consider having a stockpile of these medicines on hand at all times in the event of an emergency. No one can predict when a disaster will occur. Hospitals can be overrun with people needing critical care, and supplies can quickly disappear. Depending on the range and scope of the disaster, your ability to get a prescription filled may be limited. If the electricity was out and computers down, what would you do then?

This is a conversation I recommend you have with not only your loved ones, but also your doctor, NOW before it happens.

Evacuation Plan

There are times when you cannot shelter in place, but are forced to evacuate. Those occasions may be due to a fire or a pending storm, like a hurricane, train derailment or industrial accident. These types of events may cause you to be away from your home for either a short or long period of time. If you feel it is necessary, someone in your family needs to be assigned the task of cutting off all utilities to your home, such as your water, gas and electric. The final step before leaving your home – after securing all windows and doors of your home – is to place a laminated card on your door showing whom to contact in the event of an emergency. This should include your cell phone number as well as the designated contact person outside the area.

It is important to know in advance where you will go, how you will travel, and what routes will you take. All family members should have a pre-set designated meeting location in the event you cannot go home. Everyone should know that if home were not an option then, in the event of an emergency, everyone will meet at X location. It is important to periodically review your plans and make sure that any emergency supplies you have both at home and in your vehicles are always fresh and usable.

Closing Comments

While the thought of being prepared is not totally foreign to us, it fades quickly in importance as our everyday life gets in the way.

For the government, being prepared takes on another challenging facet. One of the greatest threats our country continues to face is war, yet technology has changed everything. Regular bombs have been replaced with nuclear devices. Also, the threats today are changing and now come within our own borders as well as being cyber based.

The protection of our leaders and, specifically, the President of the United States, has always been shrouded with a veil of secrecy for obvious reasons. As decades pass, we are now beginning to learn about secret underground bunkers and the plans that have been made in the event of a disaster and to ensure the continuity of government.

Yet, what about "we the people?" What has been done in the past and what is being done now?

Hindsight is always 20/20, and it is easy to be critical. Looking back in history, our government tried in the past to have a plan in the event of wartime to protect its citizens. First, we saw bomb shelters being built and a small amount of supplies being sent to stock those shelters. Then at the dawn of the nuclear age, realizing that those shelters could not withstand a blast, we saw that mass evacuation plans were proposed with the thought that help could be found elsewhere. Today evacuation and temporary shelters are our solution to dealing with disasters.

This begs the question: What happens if the event is so large that it encompasses not just one area or one state, but most of the country?

Under the Federal Emergency Management Agency, otherwise known as FEMA, a round of political correctness has surfaced. What was once called the National Response Plan has a new name, now called the National Response Framework. By saying you have "a plan," it leads one to think that there are specifics to follow, but using the word "framework" leaves a lot of wiggle room.

The stated mission of FEMA is: to lead America to prepare for, prevent, respond to, and recover from disasters with a vision of "A Nation Prepared." Can you think of anything the government has done recently or in the past to encourage people to really take the act of preparing seriously? Again, our everyday life struggles get in the way of most casual warnings we might hear.

Beyond yourself, do you think your neighbors are prepared? Facts show that more than 41 percent of the United States population is on at least one type of federal assistance program. According to an article from *CNN Money* dated February 2012: twenty-six percent of people in America are on Medicaid, fifteen percent on Food Stamps, eight percent on WIC, four percent on housing assistance, and two percent on temporary assistance for needy families.[64]

How much more do you think the government is capable of doing? The reality is that help is NOT necessarily on the way!

In a frequently asked questions section on the FEMA website, you can see that the key concepts of the National Response Framework have stated five principles of operation as part of the national response, which include: engaged partnerships, tiered response, scalable, flexible and adaptable operational capabilities, unity of effort through unified command, and readiness to act.[65]

It is important to note that nowhere in this statement does it say the government is going to be coming to the rescue and meet all your needs in the time of disaster. So, are people really being realistic in their thoughts about what the government is capable of doing?

The entire United States of America has identified 56,000 potential shelter facilities in the event of a disaster. These shelters would be coordinated by the Red Cross, which is a nonprofit agency and NOT an agency of the federal government. The Red Cross has a stated purpose of serving as the primary agency "to lead and coordinate efforts to provide mass care, housing, and human services after disasters that require federal assistance."

While they are chartered by Congress to provide services during a disaster, the key point often missed is that 96 percent of the total workforce for this agency is made up of volunteers! Think for a moment: if your workplace was run by all volunteers, how effective would you be at carrying out your job? I am in no way knocking the Red Cross; I think they do a wonderful and impossible job. I do, however, like to think that I am being realistic in understanding that what they can truly accomplish is limited in the face of a catastrophic disaster. Time and time again after a disaster occurs, you will read how people are disappointed that "the government" didn't do a better job at helping them.

That is why it is so important for you to be prepared NOW because when it comes to your privacy and personal security, ultimately the best chance for your survival depends on YOU!

Works Cited

1. http://www.kimberamerica.com/pepperblaster

2. http://www.taser.com/

3. http://www.aclu.org/free-speech-technology-and-liberty-womens-rights/newborn-dna-banking

4. Bamford, James. www.wired.com "The NSA Is Building the Country's Biggest Spy Center (Watch What You Say)." 15 March 2012

5. http://www.huffingtonpost.com/2013/03/13/finspy-spyware-activists_n_2864579.html

6. Ibid.

7. http://en.wikipedia.org/wiki/Fusion_center

8. http://www.brslabs.com/

9. http://www.persistentsurveillance.com

10. http://www.aao.org/newsroom/release/20130708.cfm

11. http://www.trendhunter.com/trends/biometric-eye-scan-distinctive-fingerprint-identification-iris-id-passport

12. http://gizmodo.com/5923980/the-secret-government-laser-that-instantly-knows-everything-about-you

13. http://www.retailnext.net/

14. http://www.judicialwatch.org/press-room/press-releases/jw-obtains-records-detailing-obama-administrations-warrantless-collection-of-citizens-personal-financial-data/

15. http://news.cnet.com/New-RFID-tech-would-track-airport-passengers/2100-7355_3-6125799.html

16. http://in.news.yahoo.com/lg-probes-smart-tv-snooping-allegations-104129242.html

17. http://spectrum.ieee.org/energy/policy/protecting-the-power-grid-from-solar-storms

18. http://washingtonexaminer.com/lights-out-house-plan-would-protect-nations-electricity-from-solar-flare-nuclear-bomb/article/2532038

19. http://www.nytimes.com/2013/08/17/us/as-worries-over-the-power-grid-rise-a-drill-will-simulate-a-knockout-blow.html?_r=1&

20. http://rt.com/usa/power-grid-knocked-out-substations-706/

21. http://www.computerworld.com/s/article/9233173/Timeline_Critical_infrastructure_attacks_increase_steadily_in_past_decade

22. http://www.globalresearch.ca/depositors-beware-theft-is-legal-for-big-banks-and-your-money-will-never-be-safe/5333631

23. http://www.ffiec.gov/bsa_aml_infobase/pages_manual/OLM_017.htm

24. http://www.fincen.gov/statutes_regs/guidance/pdf/msbsar_quickrefguide.pdf

25. http://www.fdic.gov/about/strategic/report/2012annualreport/index_pdf.html

26. http://www.fdic.gov/consumers/consumer/news/cnspr97/sfdpstbx.html

27. http://www.biometrics.dod.mil/

28. http://www.privacysos.org/node/926

29. http://www.fbi.gov/about-us/cjis/fingerprints_biometrics/biometric-center-of-excellence/about/about-the-biometric-center-of-excellence

30. http://www.fastcompany.com/3000272/nypd-microsoft-launch-all-seeing-domain-awareness-system-real-time-cctv-license-plate-monitoring

31. https://autos.aol.com/article/black-boxes-in-cars-will-be-standard-by-2014/

32. http://www.usatoday.com/story/news/nation/2013/12/08/cellphone-data-spying-nsa-police/3902809/

33. http://www.occupycorporatism.com/how-your-cell-phone-make-spying-easier-for-the-government-and-police/

34. http://www.postalmag.com/

35. http://www.cbsnews.com/8301-18563_162-6412439.html

36. http://theweek.com/article/index/229508/acxiom-corp-the-faceless-organization-that-knows-everything-about-you

37. http://www.experian.com/

38. http://www.forbes.com/sites/kashmirhill/2012/02/16/how-target-figured-out-a-teen-girl-was-pregnant-before-her-father-did/

39. http://www.theatlantic.com/technology/archive/2012/03/reading-the-privacy-policies-you-encounter-in-a-year-would-take-76-work-days/253851/

40. http://www.businessinsider.com/facial-recognition-technology-and-drones-2013-5

41. https://www.torproject.org/index.html.en

42. http://lifehacker.com/5505400/how-id-hack-your-weak-passwords

43. http://www.nocards.org/

44. http://www.policechiefmagazine.org/magazine/index.cfm?fuseaction=display_arch&article_id=2105&issue_id=62010

45. http://www.consumerreports.org/cro/2012/02/debunking-the-hype-over-id-theft/index.htm

46. https://www.annualcreditreport.com/cra/helpabout

47. http://www.consumer.ftc.gov/articles/0274-immediate-steps-repair-identity-theft

48. http://www.huffingtonpost.com/2012/04/11/cashless-society-week-without-cash_n_1418390.html

49. http://www.anti-climb-paint.co.uk

50. http://www.opid.org/

51. http://en.wikipedia.org/wiki/Garage_door_opener

52. http://www.cpsc.gov/en/Newsroom/News-Releases/1993/
    Safety-Commission-Publishes-Final-Rules-For-
    Automatic-Garage-Door-Openers/

53. http://www.firstwatchsecurity.com

54. http://www.poolsafely.gov/

55. http://www.usfa.fema.gov/citizens/home_fire_prev/
    electrical.shtm

56. http://www.usfa.fema.gov/citizens/home_fire_prev/
    heating/fireplace.shtm

57. http://www.usfa.fema.gov/downloads/pdf/statistics/v13i7.
    pdf

58. Ibid.

59. http://www.selfstorage.org/

60. http://travel.state.gov/travel/tips/emergencies/
    emergencies_1212.html

61. http://www.tsa.gov/traveler-information/baggage-locks

62. http://www.forbes.com/sites/andygreenberg/2012/11/26/
    security-flaw-in-common-keycard-locks-exploited-in-
    string-of-hotel-room-break-ins/

63. http://www.nrdc.org/food/files/wasted-food-ip.pdf

64. http://money.cnn.com/2012/02/07/news/economy/
    government_assistance/index.htm

65. http://www.fema.gov/pdf/emergency/nrf/NRF_FAQ.pdf

www.ingramcontent.com/pod-product-compliance
Lightning Source LLC
Chambersburg PA
CBHW070938050326

40689CB00014B/3257